The Re-Enchantment *of* Learning

A Manual for Teacher Renewal and Classroom Transformation

Sam Crowell
Renate N. Caine
Geoffrey Caine

Zephyr Press®
REACHING THEIR HIGHEST POTENTIAL
Tucson, Arizona

List of Photographic Illustrations

Original prints are available in various sizes. Please contact
Debbie Crowell
P.O. Box 1511
Idyllwild, CA 92549
(909) 659-4560

The Re-Enchantment of Learning
A Manual for Teacher Renewal and Classroom Transformation

All ages.

Printed in the United States of America

ISBN 1-56976-076-4

Editors: Veronica Durie and Stacey Shropshire
Cover design: Dan Miedaner
Photographs: Debbie Jane Crowell
Design and production: Daniel Miedaner

Zephyr Press
P.O. Box 66006
Tucson, AZ 85728-6006
http://www.zephyrpress.com

Library of Congress Cataloging-in-Publication Data

Crowell, Sam.
The re-enchantment of learning : a manual for teacher renewal and classroom transformation / Sam Crowell, Geoffrey Caine, and Renate Nummela Caine.
p. cm.
Includes bibliographical references (p.).
ISBN 1-56976-076-4
1. Teachers—United States—Handbooks, manuals, etc. 2. Teaching--United States—Handbooks, manuals, etc. I. Caine, Geoffrey.
II. Caine, Renate Nummela. III. Title.
LB1775.2.C76 1998
371.102'0973—dc21 97-25731

Contents

Preface

It was a beautiful day during late winter, with suggestions everywhere that spring was close at hand. The sky chose its bluest hue to intermingle with leafless trees and tall evergreens. The peaks of the mountains still had snow, but gentle streams and waterfalls were everywhere. It was a time of transition, change, and new beginnings. I walked silently, full of thoughts, yet open to the ongoing story nature was writing. There were truths here.

I noticed the pine needles, fallen and crunchy beneath my feet, the readiness of the seasons about to change, I could sense that nature was involved in its own process of self-transformation. A purpose and pattern engaged the entire natural system. Although not always visible or apparent, everything was participating. I felt that just being in that place made me a part of what was happening.

The air was cold on my face in contrast to the warm sun. The wind would gust forth, then fade to a quiet stillness. Yes, there were truths here.

Acknowledgments

We want to thank the educators throughout the country who have inspired us with their commitment and dedication. We hope this book honors them and provides a source of regeneration.

We especially pay tribute to the teachers and staff at Dry Creek Elementary School and those at Park View Middle School who have given so much of themselves over several years of working together with us.

We also want to express our appreciation to Bonnie Adama, Bob London, and Kerma Isaacson who provided feedback on the manuscript. Their help was invaluable.

Finally, we wish to thank so many in the Idyllwild community who constantly offered their support and encouragement. They epitomize what community is all about.

Introduction

In the fall of 1990, the three of us sat at an outdoor cafe thinking about the decade ahead of us, wondering about the years leading to a new century and a new millennium. Geoffrey and Renate had just finished a book for educators, *Making Connections: Teaching and the Human Brain* (1994) that synthesized research about how the human brain learns and what this knowledge might mean for teachers and administrators. They were awaiting its publication. Sam had recently published "A New Way of Thinking: The Challenge of the Future" (1989) in *Educational Leadership*. The article addressed the shifting emphasis in the sciences toward new questions about wholeness and relationship. We wondered if these developments might open the way to a new kind of education.

As we pondered these matters, it became clear to us that ultimately we were committed to advancing what human beings might become. Although the knowledge explosion was continuing at a relentless pace, we felt strongly that unless human beings evolved to new and greater purposes, knowledge in and of itself was ultimately not only meaningless, but dangerous. For us, learning was directly linked to expanding our possibilities as human beings, whether this expansion were to take place in classrooms, organizations, families, or as individuals. This type of personal expansion does not come merely from an accumulation of more and more knowledge; it includes an inner journey, as well. Transforming who we are, how we perceive the world, the kinds of organizations and social systems we create and live in—such are the concerns and questions that drive us. In our own unique ways, the three of us are each dedicated to this kind of work. It is the purpose behind what we do and who we are.

We finished our dinner at the cafe and, over cappucino, began discussing how we could present new information about human learning and the brain that went beyond the mere facts. The challenge was to do so in a way that would be meaningful and transforming. We sketched out ideas that would later become *MindShifts: A Brain-Based Process for Restructuring Schools and Renewing Education* (1994). In this book, we emphasized a reflective group process that helped educators understand and internalize new information about the brain and its implications for teaching and learning. We believed that there had been an overemphasis on the external nature of teaching and not enough attention given to the teacher as a person with unique strengths, beliefs, and experiences that influence the way he or she teaches. We had also observed countless efforts at reform that promoted one methodology or another, but that did not address the organizational and human factors that support prolonged growth and progress. Finally, we wanted to build upon the developmental nature of learning and the power of genuine, authentic reflection with our peers. We envisioned a discourse community supported by a group process that explores who we are, what assumptions we hold as true, how and what we teach, how we organize ourselves, and what barriers prevent us from creating authentic learning environments. Given a simple, yet sophisticated, notion of connectedness supported with a synthesis of current brain research, we wondered how educators might begin to take charge of their own growth. How would teachers individually self-organize around these ideas and what would the schools they created look like?

Since that evening, we have had the opportunity to work with many teachers and administrators and to find some answers to our initial questions. We have tied our understandings to newer research in complex adaptive systems, complexity theory, and other new sciences. We have implemented these ideas and watched schools change and grow in unique ways while exhibiting a common bond that is undeniable. We have seen administrators at every level change the way they conceive of their work and become completely different as organizational leaders. We have watched teachers transform their lives both outside and inside the classroom; they inspire the people around them with their genuine and sincere thirst for learning and personal growth. We have witnessed students achieving well above their grade level, but more importantly, engaging active and personal interest in learning. We have also found ourselves on a journey that has consumed us; it has led us beyond education and organizational development to a consideration of the broader dimensions of human consciousness and our part in the cosmic picture. We have found many, many educators who find in our work something that resonates deeply within them. They have come to us with words of gratitude, tears of emotion, sparkling eyes of wonder and curiosity. They tell their own stories and share the intuitive truths from their experience. They inspire us and touch us with the soulful nature of their dedication and commitment. It is good to know that many of us share similar journeys. Although our steps are small, each step creates a broader and more recognizable path.

We don't present these observations as promises, but rather as evidence that real transformations can happen. When we change the nature of our assumptions about what education has to be, tap the inner creativity that we all possess, and create a professional community different from what we have been used to, the entire substance and activity of education can be different. We are not idealistic—we've been involved with schools for too long not to be aware of the realities and problems that schools face. What we have noticed, though, is that technical "solutions" and instructional panaceas by themselves don't work. Don't misunderstand, there are many fine programs and innovations, but year after year, in-service after in-service, schools find themselves fighting many of the same battles and basically operating in the same way. There is a missing element in most of these efforts—they do not address the inner consciousness of teachers and school communities.

We are convinced that most teachers want a coherent picture of the learning and teaching process, which they can use to create a stronger, more substantive curriculum and to enliven the instructional processes they choose. These changes can't be made overnight; they involve a journey of self-discovery and a new way of perceiving our task. Admittedly not everyone is ready for this journey, but those who are will find that it is a journey of meaning and possibility. This book is our attempt to create experiences and understandings to help you along the journey.

Why This Book Was Written

This book is meant to be a process book. What we mean is that we have written the book not to be read for information, but to be read for reflection and action. There is information here that we hope is interesting, significant, and valuable. But our purpose is for you to go more deeply into what the information might mean for you—in your personal life, your professional practice, and your school environment. It is a book about possibility and it is this sense of possibility that we hope to engage in you.

Our work in schools has centered upon making theory come to life. We have established process groups that journey together into questions about their thinking and practice and who commit to creating together a kind of school that reflects their deepest understandings about learning and growth. We have found that through process groups, school communities can tap the collective power of imagination and support. We mention this process throughout the book and provide a process guide in the appendix. We hope you will take advantage of the opportunity to create a group at your school, using this book as a resource. It has been our experience that taking this initiative is a way to grow most dramatically in our own practice and to sustain larger school transitions based on a coherent though ever-changing vision.

Two recent books by Renate and Geoffrey have articulated the need for a new examination of our assumptions about schooling. The books are based on insights from the new sciences of complex adaptive systems and on an emerging worldview or paradigm that expands our understanding of nature and challenges our previous ways of thinking. These ideas have an impact on virtually every discipline, as well as on the institutions and practices that were founded on an earlier worldview. The scope of these changes is larger than any particular philosophy or theory; these ideas have the power to reorganize an entire culture.

Understanding the implications of such sweeping changes involves perceiving the world in a way different from the worldview you may currently hold. In order to move beyond where we are in education, we will need to be able to think, perceive, and act with a new sense of understanding about the world. Suzi Gablik (1983) states that "the way to prepare the ground for a new paradigm is to make changes in one's own life" (8). But what kinds of changes are required? How do they relate to our teaching and our schools? Some answers to these questions are provided in Renate and Geoffrey's book, *Unleashing the Power of Perceptual Change: The Promise of Brain-Based Teaching* (1997b). In that book the relationship between instructional approaches and what the Caines call "perceptual orientations" is made clear. They identify and describe characteristics of three orientations that reflect the way we perceive the educational process and how we teach. What they call Orientation Three thinking requires a fundamental shift, not just in how we think, but in who we are as teachers. We hope this book becomes a pathway to a journey of deeper understanding of Orientation Three thinking and living it in the classroom.

We have found an eagerness on the part of many teachers and administrators to create exciting and dynamic classrooms and schools that focus on both substantive learning and creativity. There is a point, however, at

> *The purpose of this book is to help those teachers and administrators move through the threshold of their own thinking.*

which many of these teachers and administrators become stalled. They push ahead with one new method after another but cannot seem to get to where they want to go. We have observed that those who were able to break through whatever limitation was holding them back ultimately had to reconsider some of the fundamental aspects of teaching and learning they were holding on to. Primarily it was their thinking, not their skills, that was holding them back. The purpose of this book is to help those teachers and administrators move through the threshold of their own thinking.

We know that this book will not speak to everyone in the same way, for it places teaching within a context that has not been addressed before now. For many, however, we hope that it provides information, experiences, explanations, and process reflections that will empower your own responses and creativity. It is a journey to Orientation Three thinking.

What "Reenchantment of Learning" Means

Both teaching and learning are part of our very humanity. They must somehow address who we are, not just what we know. Knowing cannot be isolated from a sense of self or from a sense of meaning and purpose. Thomas Moore (1992) said it well: "As long as we leave care of the soul out of our daily lives we will suffer the loneliness of living in a dead, cold, unrelated world. We can 'improve' ourselves to the maximum, and yet we will still feel the alienation inherent in a divided existence. We will continue to exploit nature and our capacity to invent new things, but both will continue to overpower us, if we do not approach them with enough depth and imagination" (284). If teaching and learning are extricated from who we are as individuals, from our hopes and dreams, from our visions of a different kind of world for ourselves and our children, and from our belief that there is a special significance to each of our lives, then it will be doomed as a sterile activity with only short-term, instrumental purposes.

As we have worked with teachers, we have noticed they have a hunger to acknowledge the human qualities of their work. In some of our group processes, teachers have broken down and cried, saying that it was the first time in years someone had really listened to them. These experiences suggest to us that there is a spirit behind what each of us does that needs to be nourished and supported. We also believe that it needs to be unleashed. We hope this book elevates the connection between who we are as persons and who we are as teachers.

The concept of "reenchantment" is rooted in the evolution of human thought. There was a time in human history that our species felt a greater part of the wonder and creation of Earth. We felt a sense of connectedness and an inherent relationship with all things. We saw ourselves as an integral part of the universe. Many indigenous peoples still maintain this sense of relatedness.

A conceptual revolution took place almost four hundred years ago that ultimately changed the way we view the world. It was the birth of modern science, and it provided a way to think that allowed us to maximize our ability to control the material world. As a result, we have learned over the centuries to perceive that world as objective phenomena, to be acted upon and used for our benefit. We have developed a kind of faith in scientism that somehow we can "fix" any problem by using new technologies and methods.

Over time many modern cultures no longer viewed themselves as an integral part of nature, but rather, removed from it, and in a peculiar way, removed from one another as well. All of our modern institutions were built upon the ideas that characterize this perception of the world. The problems we face today and many of the problems confronting all our institutions stem from the limitations of these ideas. They are so pervasive and so much a part of us we don't even recognize their existence. As the world becomes more and more complex and interconnected, these ideas not only will be less useful, but they may threaten our very survival.

Ironically, the science that was created by this perception of the world is also bringing it into question. The "new sciences," as they are called, describe a different kind of reality, one that is inherently connected, relational, interwoven, holistic. It is more ecological and perceives the world contextually. It shows the limitations of external control and focuses instead on questions of self-reference and self-organization. These ideas provide more insight into a complex world.

In a strange way, these ideas also return us to a time of earlier human traditions. Whereas the modernist worldview addresses only an external reality, the new sciences focus on the interaction between the internal and the external. Questions of spirit and consciousness are entertained on the periphery of this science.

Reenchantment, then, is a recognition that brings "self" and our relationship with Earth back into focus. It is not about going back to a different time or creating an unworkable fantasy; rather it is about regaining a sense of connection and seeing that we are part of a greater whole. This sense of connection, if embedded deeply into the fabric of our living, changes our approach to life, provides a kind of peace and harmony, and urges us to live actively in the world. It also changes the way we conceive of teaching and learning.

It is the power of learning that we want to bring alive in ourselves and in the lives of our students. Real learning goes beyond facts and information and affects our very being. The question becomes "How can learning help us transcend our old notions of who we are and lead us to the edge of possibility?"

How the Book Is Organized

The Re-Enchantment of Learning is organized into four parts, each with a separate focus. Part 1 is an important commentary that summarizes what brain-based teaching is and how it provides a coherent learning theory upon which any teacher or school can build. In addition, this part explains why our present assumptions are no longer adequate. It introduces the new landscape of ideas that we must eventually come to understand. Each of us is placed at the threshold of a "new beginning" that offers both possibility and hope. Part 1 is the foundation of the practice described in this book.

Each of us is placed at the threshold of a "new beginning" that offers both possibility and hope.

Part 2 engages us in perceiving the world in terms of our relationship with it. It reclaims values that are part of our human heritage—joy, connectedness, wonder, awe, and imagination. The emphasis of part 2 is on our ability to "see" the world in a different way and to begin to apply these perceptions to classroom practice.

Part 3 helps us approach our teaching as Orientation Three thinkers. It assists us in making the transition from perceiving to doing. We begin to apply our understandings in the classroom. These skills include an expansion of cognitive horizons or being able to see the bigger picture in what we teach. It leads us to see ourselves as empowered decision makers who in turn have the ability to empower our students. It helps us understand the nature of process as a context for both instruction and school transformation.

Part 4 reminds us that for learning to be meaningful, it must be responsive. Responsive learning is that which draws upon the interests and expressive qualities of the student; it is also that learning which takes action in the world around us. Responsive learning draws us inward to tap the originality and creativity of thought and understanding. It also draws us outward, asking us what the responsibility of our knowing is, what kind of people we will be.

> *Shifting perceptions . . . is a process that is rooted in reflection, awareness, and community.*

To get the most from this book, we recommend that you read it through first individually. You may want to try some of the personal reflective processes that are provided at the end of each chapter. We suggest that you then read it as a group, using the group process from the beginning. We have conceived of this book as a six month process, so we recommend that you take your time, considering one chapter at every group meeting. Each chapter contains information as well as stories, and occasionally, poetry. We want to engage your heart as well as your mind. Reflective processes at the end of each chapter are designed to explore your own thinking in greater depth. These processes are a significant part of the book because through them we are able to confront some of the difficult questions educators must ask while giving you an opportunity to experience the book at a deeper level. The activities will engage you in an ongoing practice. We use the word "practice" in the sense of a path toward personal mastery. Developing a practice helps us gain an almost intuitive understanding of what we are doing. We hope to lead you to this understanding.

We have found that shifting our perceptions takes time. It is a process that is rooted in reflection, awareness, and community. Once our perceptions of the world are changed, they have ramifications in every area of our lives. This book is for those who are serious about beginning that journey. We wish you well.

Part 1

Beginning the Journey

> *Each of us begins somewhere. Each day is an adventure in possibility, where the future comes together with the past, and the potential of who we are waits to be created.*

Part 1 provides an overview of a brain-based theory of learning and a brief exploration of the intellectual roots of "reenchantment." This groundwork is essential as a context for the rest of the chapters. We have found that this understanding helps to loosen the shackles that often hold us in untenable ways of viewing learning and teaching. As Mark Engel states, "for us to change our perception-determining beliefs, we must first become aware that reality is not necessarily as we believe it to be" (in Bateson 1974, vii). This process is not always easy, but we may have no choice but to go through it if we are to grow as teachers. It is clear to us that education cannot remain as it is.

We feel that teaching and learning are creative, intellectual, practical, and spiritual activities. Their effects do not go away and their impact may be among the most significant in life. We have observed firsthand the flowering of self-confidence, intellect, and creativity among teachers who take the first steps to view their practice differently from the traditional. We have seen their students achieve and grow in ways that seem only natural. We have watched parents cry for joy at the unexpected levels of their children's accomplishments. These experiences are real to us and are not just inert ideas.

We hope that part 1 functions as a kind of trail marker. It is a place to begin, to engage our intellect, and to prepare ourselves for the journey ahead. The path is not a quick one, but it promises many vistas, some wonderful experiences along the way, and an opportunity to choose our own direction.

Each of us begins somewhere. Each day is an adventure in possibility, where the future comes together with the past, and the potential of who we are waits to be created. Life is connected in ways we do not fully understand, but more and more we are discovering that these connections may be the heart and soul of who we are.

Beginnings

1

Beginning a Search for *New Possibilities*

> *I have always known*
> *That at last I would*
> *Take this road, but yesterday*
> *I did not know that it would be today.*
>
> —Narihira

This particular chapter will provide a background for learning and teaching based on brain research and its implications. It will summarize the continuum of instructional strategies that we have observed as teachers move through this process. Finally, and most importantly, we will discuss the orientations toward teaching that shape the very essence of teachers' practice. What we have termed Orientation Three thinking requires a fundamental shift in the way we view the world. It is one thing to understand the nature of this changed worldview intellectually; it is quite another to live it. This book is about a journey to Orientation Three thinking. It is not information about teaching; rather, it is an exploration of how we can be different kinds of teachers. For us, the reenchantment of learning is a journey to becoming Orientation Three teachers and learners.

Why Is a New Approach to Learning Important?

Our dominant approach to learning and teaching is through what is called the "delivery method." We package and deliver information using the best means we know. Most educators spend a great deal of time planning how to deliver information in the most effective and efficient ways, which is a growing challenge as the needs and backgrounds of our students become more acute and diverse. In addition, we have to deal with the increasing demands of a complex society, a dramatically changing world, and a virtual transformation of many of our disciplines. It isn't that the delivery of information is bad, but that it is becoming increasingly limited as a model for education.

If we listen to the public, they not only want higher standards and a strong foundation in traditional knowledge, they also want students to be creative, analytical, and ready for the reality of the work world. Even in the most prestigious schools, both public and private, there is little success in meeting all these demands, especially for all students.

Most educators we know tend to believe that the problem is in the demands themselves. It isn't that they don't agree with all of these goals, but be reasonable! Given the time, resources, and the needs of their students, they can only do so much. It is as if teachers are always struggling just to keep up. Often when they do respond and regroup for one kind of emphasis or another, the issue changes again and they are back where they started. And so it goes.

But is the problem really in the demands? Could it be that students can actually do much more than they are currently doing and be more creative in the process? Could it be that learning can be much more meaningful and relate more directly to the entire growth process of an individual? Is the delivery model that we have come to identify as what teachers do actually part of the problem? If we could get outside the box of the delivery model concept, would there be new possibilities for an expanded notion of what learning really is?

The three of us believe that the delivery model is useful in fewer and fewer situations, and for many kinds of learning it may serve to impede the scope and the substance of what might be learned. We are also observing that technology is rapidly being developed and used that has the capability of "delivering" information more rapidly, more extensively, and more efficiently than many teachers. This phenomenon is making the privatization of education look very attractive to several large corporations. We are not suggesting that teachers are unimportant or obsolete, or that machines can take the place of people. We are saying, however, that if delivering information is all teaching is about, then we may want to reconsider our purpose as educators. We may also want to reconsider whether the delivery model is best suited for the complex demands of a new millennium. Unless learning can be redefined to include the tapping of the creative potential of the human spirit and the unleashing of our ability to transcend our finite conceptions of self, then we wonder what the accumulation of more and more information is all about. Based on what we are learning about the brain, we believe that it is possible to accomplish the accumulation of information *and* the expansion of the boundaries of our humanness.

Three Kinds of Knowing

Kevin Kelly (1994) writes that "investing machines with the ability to adapt on their own, to evolve in their own direction, and grow without human oversight is the next great advance in technology" (127). Why are we saying this about machines and not about human beings? We cannot cynically give up on our humanity. We cannot reverse roles with our machines, giving them the opportunities of the human legacy and relegating to ourselves the sterile role of technician. We do not mean to denigrate our technological accomplishments or to create a *we* versus *them*. We are saying only that learning is meant to empower our full humanity, and for it to do so, we must go beyond the delivery model and the current purposes of most of our educational enterprises.

When the three of us talk about learning, we generally have three kinds of knowledge in mind. The first is *surface* knowledge. Most of our textbooks are good examples of this type of knowledge. It is usually a sweeping coverage of facts and information, major terms and concepts, and broad summaries of theories. Names, dates, or major categories may also be included, with indications of what the experts consider most significant. In most cases this kind of knowledge is dealt with as an isolated collection of information. It is rarely connected to any other purpose other than "you should know it" or "you need it to graduate." Students may be able to do very well in such courses and still have little or no understanding about the subject. Curriculum guides at every grade level are filled with surface knowledge expectations that each teacher is suppose to "cover." Students often find this kind of knowledge dreadfully boring and if they do not buy into the system, they struggle just to endure it. Many students from various ethnic and cultural backgrounds perceive this knowledge as "white knowledge" because it requires them to learn only about the mainstream culture and to relate facts that may be in direct contrast to what they believe. Thus they are asked to relinquish their cultural identity in order to succeed. Whether their perception is accurate or not, it is a barrier for many in our schools.

A second kind of knowledge we discuss is *technical* or *scholastic* knowledge. This kind of knowledge is more skill based and places a greater emphasis on depth and relationship. We begin to understand the inner workings of the chosen discipline and we can see how the particular concepts and theories make use of the information and facts. What we learn has greater internal consistency and significance. This kind of knowledge, however, rarely goes outside its disciplinary boundaries, and a student often does not know how the subject relates to any other subject except in the most general way. There is also little participation in the discipline itself; there is only more substantive knowledge about the discipline. Many do not understand that a discipline is not just something one knows about, but it is primarily a creative activity in which one participates.

While we note the usefulness of both surface and technical or scholastic knowledge, we are much more interested in what we call *dynamical* knowledge. *Dynamical* is a technical term that is used to describe open systems. This knowledge comes alive for us. We play with it, experiment with it, and participate voluntarily in learning more specifics and sharing our discoveries. In ordinary life, we often experience dynamical knowledge most naturally in our absorption in hobbies, special interests, or creative activities. A discipline's language becomes second nature. Your interest is sparked by the smallest detail and the opportunity to pursue a new question or experiment with methodology is widely encouraged. One begins to identify with one's participation in the subject matter and to carve out an expertise that is unique and valued. The big picture is clearly perceived, as are relationships among related disciplines. What is significant about dynamical knowledge is that we participate in it. We use surface and technical knowledge to pursue new and creative questions. We develop an expertise that becomes part of us. Dynamical knowledge is found in the process of learning the subtleties of a profession. It becomes part of our work personality. We believe that dynamical knowledge should be a significant part of every student's experience at all levels of schooling. If we as teachers aim for "learners as experts," the three of us believe there will be a new kind of energy throughout education.

This task seems daunting, given the kind of delivery model that is so firmly established. But in this area, a new understanding of the brain can perhaps help us the most. The brain principles, consolidated by Renate and Geoffrey from many areas of current research, begin to deepen our understanding of accomplishing all three kinds of knowledge, while emphasizing the significance of meaning and purpose in learning. This is quite a claim, we know! It is often at this point that many educators say, "Wait a minute. I'm not sure I want to invest time and energy in one more fad." We actually agree. What we call, for lack of a better term, *brain-based learning* is really a process of making natural, self-determined changes in the learning environment, our teaching, and our curriculum that reflect a deepened understanding of how we learn and what learning is. We have had teachers tell us that for the first time they know why they do what they do. Others have stated that they now see many of the programs in which they have been in-serviced in terms of a bigger picture or umbrella. Brain-based learning is not a recipe of how-to's. It gives the power to teachers and schools to apply a deeper understanding of natural learning and create opportunities for this learning to occur. For our purposes, it also extends beyond knowing. It raises significant questions about the deeper meanings of life and being.

What Are the Brain-Based Principles?

The following principles of learning are based on a synthesis of research from the fields of neuroscience, physiology, optimal performance studies, neuropsychology, stress management, psychology, and more. Most of this research has been slow to find its way in any coherent form to educators. What the Caines have done is to make available research that is particularly relevant to educators. What sometimes may appear to be common sense often reflects subtleties and understandings that have significant implications not previously developed. Elaboration and applications of these principles can be found in *Making Connections* (1994), *MindShifts* (1994), and *Education on the Edge of Possibility* (1997).

1. The brain is a complex adaptive system.

Perhaps the most potent feature of the brain is its capacity to function simultaneously on many levels and in many ways, which is one reason we have combined two principles (the brain is a parallel processor and learning engages the entire physiology). Thoughts, emotions, imagination, predispositions, and physiology operate interactively as the entire system interacts with and exchanges information with its environment. Moreover, there are emergent properties of the brain as a whole system that cannot be recognized nor understood when isolated parts are explored. Education *must* come to terms with the multifaceted nature of the human learner.

2. The brain is a social brain.

We begin to be shaped as our immensely receptive brains/minds interact with our very early environment and within relationships. Vygotsky is partially responsible for noting the connection between social interaction and knowledge. Throughout our lives, our brains/minds change in response to their engagement with others—so much so that individuals must always be seen to be integral parts of larger social systems. Indeed, part of our identity depends on establishing community and finding ways to belong. Learning, therefore, is profoundly influenced by the nature of social relationships.

3. **The search for meaning is innate.**

   "The search for meaning" refers generally to making sense of our experiences. This search is survival oriented and basic to the human brain/mind. While the ways in which we make sense of our experience change over time, the central drive to do so does not. At its core, the search for meaning is purpose and value driven. Maslow noted the extent of this human search. Included are such basic questions as "Who am I?" and "Why am I here?" The search for meaning ranges from the need to eat and find safety through the development of relationships and a sense of identity to an exploration of our potential and the quest for transcendence.

4. **The search for meaning occurs through patterning.**

   Patterning includes innate and acquired schematic maps and categories. The brain/mind needs and automatically registers the familiar while searching for and responding to novel stimuli. Therefore, the brain/mind is both scientist and artist, discerning and understanding patterns as they occur and giving expression to unique and creative patterns of its own. It resists having meaninglessness imposed on it. By *meaninglessness,* we mean isolated pieces of information unrelated to what makes sense to a particular learner. Effective education must give learners an opportunity to formulate their own patterns of understanding.

5. **Emotions are critical to patterning.**

   What we learn is influenced and organized by emotions and mind-sets involving expectancy, personal biases, self-esteem, and the need for social interaction. Emotions and thoughts shape each other and cannot be separated. Emotions color meaning. The emotional impact of any lesson or life experience may continue to reverberate long after the specific event that triggers it. An appropriate emotional climate is indispensable to sound education.

6. **Every brain simultaneously perceives and creates parts and wholes.**

   Although there is some truth to the "left-brain/right-brain" distinction, it does not tell the whole story. In a healthy person, both hemispheres interact in every activity, from art and computing to sales and accounting. The two-brain doctrine is most useful for reminding us that the brain reduces information into parts while perceiving holistically. Good training and education recognize this phenomenon, for example by introducing natural global projects and ideas from the beginning.

7. **Learning involves focused attention and peripheral perception.**

   The brain absorbs information of which it is directly aware, but it also directly absorbs information that lies beyond its immediate attention. In fact, it responds to the larger sensory context in which teaching and communication occur. "Peripheral signals" are extremely potent. Even the unconscious signals that reveal our inner beliefs have a powerful impact on students. Educators should pay extensive attention to all facets of the educational environment.

8. **Learning always involves conscious and unconscious processes.**

   One aspect of consciousness is awareness. Much of our learning is unconscious in that experience and sensory input is processed below the level of awareness, which means that much understanding may *not* occur during a class but hours, weeks, or months later. It also means that educators must organize what they do so as to facilitate that subsequent unconscious processing of experience by students. In practice, this organization includes proper design of the context, the incorporation of reflection and metacognitive activities, and the incorporation of methods to help learners creatively elaborate on the ideas, skills, and experiences. Teaching largely becomes a matter of helping learners make visible what is invisible.

9. **We have at least two ways of organizing memory.**

   Although there are many models of memory, one that provides an excellent platform for educators is the distinction made by O'Keefe and Nadel (1978) between taxon and locale memories. They suggest that we have a set of systems for recalling relatively unrelated information (taxon systems, from *taxonomies*). These systems are motivated by reward and punishment. They suggest that we also have a spatial and autobiographical memory that does not need rehearsal and allows for instant recall of experiences. This system registers the details of your meal last night. It is always engaged, inexhaustible, and motivated by novelty. Thus we are biologically supplied with the capacity to register complete experiences. It is through a combination of both approaches to memory that meaningful learning occurs. Thus meaningful and meaningless information are organized and stored differently.

10. Learning is developmental.

Development occurs in several ways. In part, the brain is plastic, which means that much of its hard wiring is shaped by the experiences that people have. In part, there are predetermined sequences of development in childhood, including windows of opportunity for laying down the basic hardware necessary for later learning. For this reason, new languages and the arts ought to be introduced to children very early in life. Finally, in many respects, there is no limit to growth and to the capacities of humans to learn more. Neurons continue to be capable of making new connections throughout life.

11. Complex learning is enhanced by challenge and inhibited by threat.

The brain/mind learns optimally—that is, it makes maximum connections—when appropriately challenged in an environment that encourages taking risks. However, the brain/mind downshifts under perceived threat. It then becomes less flexible and reverts to primitive attitudes and procedures. We must create and maintain an atmosphere of relaxed alertness that involves low threat and high challenge. However, low threat is *not* synonymous with simply feeling good. The essential element of perceived threat is a feeling of helplessness or fatigue. Occasional stress and anxiety are inevitable in genuine learning because genuine learning involves changes that lead to a reorganization of the self. Such learning can be intrinsically stressful, irrespective of the skill of, and support offered by, a teacher.

12. Every brain is uniquely organized.

We all have the same set of systems, yet we are all different. Some of this difference is a consequence of our genetic endowment; some of it is a consequence of different environments and experiences. The differences express themselves in terms of learning styles, differing talents and intelligences, and so on. An important corollary is both to appreciate that learners are different and need choices while ensuring that they are exposed to a multiplicity of inputs. Multiple intelligences and vast ranges or diversity are, therefore, characteristic of what it means to be human.

From Learning to Teaching

Many programs will claim to have a brain-based approach. They go under the titles of Accelerated Learning, Optimal Learning, Quantum Learning, imaging and visualization techniques, as well as alternative approaches directed at learning through our unconscious. While not all of these approaches would be acceptable in schools, they nonetheless have a growing record of success. In general, they all are oriented toward faster and more effective memorization of facts and relationships. We do not disparage these kinds of instructional applications. In fact, we use some of them ourselves. What we do want to point out, however, is that only in those instances where they go beyond the delivery model of instruction and its overwhelming focus on surface knowledge do they begin to touch on what we mean by *brain based*.

We believe that to use brain-based principles only for learning surface knowledge is to fail to take advantage of the far-reaching implications for learning that these principles represent. Our aim is to address the systemic challenges in education today and deal with the nature of meaning, creativity, self-efficacy, and dynamical knowledge. We believe that real learning should transcend the limited categories that most schools have established. Real learning is not only about knowing more "stuff," it is also about expanding the possibilities of our human potential and understanding our relationship with the world beyond ourselves.

An Instructional Model to Guide Teachers

To assist teachers in putting the brain principles into practice, we offer three broad areas of emphasis. Relaxed alertness, orchestrated immersion in complex experiences, and active processing. *Relaxed alertness* refers to a state of mind that allows optimal performance and to the creation of an environment that supports this condition. These conditions require the absence of threat but the presence of challenge. Learners experience a personal buy-in to the challenge and have a foundation of readiness. In addition, the learner is physically relaxed and open to expend energy toward a focused and purposeful goal. An analogy for this state of mind and physical readiness is the champion athlete. You will often hear commentators note that a successful runner has an easy, relaxed stride or a struggling runner is tense and tight. Optimal performance literature suggests that a relaxed and ready state of mind is essential to achieve and maintain high levels of performance.

We know that limited time parameters, threat of punishment, or even the promise of reward can be as debilitating as they are motivational. What appears to be more important is the significance of the task and the combination of confident readiness and challenge; there is purposefulness in what students are doing and they can understand it in terms of their own interests and experience. As part of the brain-based instructional model, we give significant attention to creating the kinds of environments that foster relaxed alertness.

The second emphasis in this model is *orchestrated immersion in complex experiences*. We learn best when we are immersed in multilayered experiences that allow us to recognize relevant patterns and see their connections.

This immersion allows learners to see the connections between the big picture and the minute parts. Themes, significant projects, and purposeful, real-life experience are some typical ways you can orchestrate this immersion.

Orchestrated immersion is a way to create a context that embeds specific brain principles in the learning environment. There is no one way to do this. Rather, it requires constant ingenuity and creativity. Emphasis is on information and creativity, analysis and application, conceptual understanding and personal meaning. Our integration skills need to be greatly refined. Abilities to embed the particular in the global, the abstract in the concrete, the analytical in the creative need significant attention.

A key to orchestrated immersion is that it involves complex experiences. We perceive experience as a whole and if we want substantive learning to occur, then the context of experience must be rich and powerful. Authentic, complex experience offers the learner and the educator infinite possibilities for significant learning. The teacher, however, must be able to help students glean information, skills, value lessons, and concepts that present themselves as parts of many wholes rather than as separate and isolated attributes, which suggests an orientation for what we as educators do that is different from what we have done in the past.

A third and essential emphasis is called *active processing*. It refers to the ways we process or learn from our experience. Some of this processing we do naturally, but the frontier of learning and of realizing an expanded human potential lies, we believe, in the deepening quality of reflective processing. From the simple question "What did you learn from this?" to a complex investigation of meaning and significance through a creative and personal application, active processing provides an opportunity for meaning making. It is both contemplative and interactive. It is found in the quality of our questions, the substance of our feedback, and the permission to explore beyond the borders of disciplines and the conventional. It is a focusing on who we are as much as what we know. Active processing assists the teacher in perceiving every experience as a learning opportunity and as a way to a greater awareness of our external and internal universe.

Instructional Approaches and Perceptual Orientations

Over the years of introducing these ideas and practices to teachers, we have found that not only do teachers have different styles, but they differ significantly in what they perceive to be their roles as teachers. These perceptions are usually only loosely defined and they serve to constitute ways to organize and approach what teachers do. Instructionally, these perceptions deal with the way teachers define in practice the objective of instruction;

the use of time; the source of curriculum; their definition and application of discipline; and their approach to assessment.

In *Unleashing the Power of Perceptual Change* (1997b), Renate and Geoffrey deal at length with the significance of these distinctions. Our purpose here is merely to identify the distinctions as Instructional Approach One, Instructional Approach Two, and Instructional Approach Three. Broadly, the instructional approaches move from being primarily teacher controlled using a delivery model to being primarily learner centered, with a high degree of student participation and student decision making in a dynamic learning environment. It is important to note that we perceive all three of these approaches to be necessary and useful, depending on the context. Each instructional approach, however, requires different kinds of skills and, more importantly, different ways of thinking. For example, we have found that Instructional Approach Three teachers (those who are most flexible and have organic classroom environments) are able to use all three instructional approaches as they find it necessary or useful. Instructional Approach One teachers, however, find it difficult to move into Instructional Approach Two and have almost no conception or interest in Instructional Approach Three. In other words, they cannot move constructively out of the delivery model without experiencing an almost total breakdown of order and learning. Instructional Approach Two teachers, on the other hand, have adapted well to greater classroom interaction, drawing on student interests and abilities. Their classrooms typically emphasize relationship and free-flowing discussion. These teachers often feel caught between delivering on content and providing more complex and authentic experiences. They may mistakenly perceive that engagement in activity is the same as learning and find themselves vacillating between instructional approaches one and two. Teaching at Instructional Approach Three is not necessarily only intuited, it can be learned.

Our observation is that the distinctions among these approaches are both developmental and perceptual. There are indeed different kinds of skills and techniques that allow one to be successful at each instructional level. More significantly, however, there are different assumptions about the nature of learning, the role of teaching, and what it means to realize our human potential. These assumptions are not just differences in philosophy; they are deeply embedded in the ways we perceive the world and our places in it. We call these perceptual orientations. They have an impact on everything we do and they help define the possibilities of who we might become.

As our perceptions shift, so do our capacities to adopt different instructional approaches. Our emphasis, then, is to create transitions in our perceptual orientations. While we identify three, the heart of our work is in the development of Orientation Three teachers. We have found the perceptual categories (described in detail in Caine and Caine 1997a) supported in principle by other thinkers and researchers (Bateson 1974; Harmon 1988; Miller 1993). The following descriptions give some flavor to what we mean by Orientation Three.

1. Orientation Three thinkers' primary objective is a deeper awareness and sense of self. They notice that everything we do is the proper object of our attention and awareness.
2. Orientation Three thinkers see power as residing within each of us and not in external forces or authority figures. They believe in their ability to effect change.
3. Orientation Three thinkers perceive the relationships between information and experience, between learning and context, and between students and teacher.
4. Orientation Three thinkers have a sense of wholeness and interconnectedness. They can see more connections among and between subjects, disciplines, and life. They have a capacity for seeing the bigger picture.

The essence of Orientation Three is not what we know but what we are becoming; our capacity to perceive ourselves and the world in more expansive terms; and the ability to experience life with wholeness, joy, wonder, and a sense of connectedness. We believe these purposes resonate with calls for reenchantment, for a reconnection, albeit perhaps a connection through a different method, to the soulful nature of our being as well as our intellect.

We are at a place in human history when the very conception of the world itself is changing. The nature of knowledge, our relationship with Earth and with one another, our capacity for meaning and creativity are all part of an impending transition taking place within every discipline, within social and organizational systems, and within the consciousness of humans throughout the world.

The rest of this book is a journey toward an enlivening of the human spirit. It is a journey to Orientation Three thinking as we explore the wonders of a new perceptual landscape. It is our hope that in perceiving a world of new possibilities, you will experience for yourself the reenchantment of learning.

Process and Reflections

We want to introduce here the procedures for the group process. Later chapters will go beyond the group process to include suggested personal reflections and applications to teaching. If you are reading this by yourself, we suggest that you use the reflective questions that follow to explore the ideas in this chapter more deeply. It may be helpful also to get an idea now of what we mean by *group process.*

Please practice the group process outlined in the appendix. We have a great deal of confidence in this process and have tested it over time. Notice that it will require practice and may feel artificial at first. It also requires respect for "borders," such as beginnings and endings. At the same time that the procedures may feel confining, the point is to develop a flow in our thinking that is as free and open as possible. This process does not include an agenda or to-do list. If at all possible, stay with the topics or questions selected and finish work-related issues or left over to-do items before you begin, or reserve them for after the group has finished.

We begin by developing some basic agreements with group members before beginning and developing coherent procedures that ultimately allow for the greatest degree of authenticity and openness. Besides clear procedures, other elements of low threat should include seeing ourselves as continuous learners, not individuals searching for the "right" thing to say or the "perfect" answer. We strongly recommend that the group adhere to Carl Rogers's (1969) three elements for personal growth, which include empathy for self and others, authenticity with self and others, and respect for one's own journey of learning and the learning of others. These elements create a low-threat or trusting environment that serves as the heart of learning and an emergent process on the road to reenchantment.

We also suggest that you make a habit of checking assumptions—your own and those of your colleagues. Assumptions give us an insight into our own and others' mental models. They are often so deep that we are unaware of them. Hence we need to learn how to master the art of self-reflection. Assumptions do not need to be defended, just brought into the light to be aired and understood. By looking at our assumptions in a nonjudgmental way, we open a path to genuine dialogue and understanding. Chapter 8 deals with additional abilities you may need to develop as time goes on, such as conflict resolution and "I" messages.

Once you have your process in place, begin by choosing to focus on some of the following issues and questions:

1. It is important to develop a common vocabulary. On the surface, doing so may sound easy, but if you check individual and group assumptions, you may find that words you thought everyone perceived in the same way actually carry very different meanings for different individuals. Make sure the following words and phrases are clear and that you all agree on what the meanings are:

Self-discovery *Learning*
Ways of perceiving *Human spirit*

2. Do the concepts *surface knowledge, technical* or *scholastic knowledge,* and *dynamical knowledge* make sense? How comfortable are you using these terms? Will you be able to use these terms in future discussions, linking them to common meanings and assumptions? What do you need in order to do so?
3. When we speak of *threat,* we are not referring to anxiety or feeling nervous about something. We are referring to anxiety accompanied by a sense of helplessness. *High challenge,* on the other hand, refers to the learner's deep commitment and interest, sparked by a sense of belief in the ability to succeed. How do you collectively and individually understand *low threat* and *high challenge*?
4. How and when do threat and challenge differ and play a role in your teaching or your own learning and the learning of your community?
5. What do we mean when we say that teachers who do brain-based teaching need to be able to master three interactive elements: relaxed alertness, immersion in complex experience, and active processing? What examples and possibilities of these three are there? What do you need in order to understand these concepts more clearly?
6. What role does perception play in reenchantment? Do you agree that our perceptions influence what we do? How does self-discovery relate? Does it?
7. Either individually or in a group, think of examples outside of formal educational settings where you have experienced the brain-based principles. Think beyond the examples to the feelings and emotions that were present. What took place? How did you feel? Principles, because of their general nature, can be easily dismissed. Get behind the words to what they really might mean.
8. Use the principles to analyze specific activities in your own classroom. Think about them in relation to what happens or does not happen. What if you used the principles to optimize what you do? What might change? What might you do more of? Less of? Differently? What new skills might you need?
9. Choose one or two principles and consciously use them to reflect on your teaching over the course of several days.
10. Consider your curriculum in terms of surface knowledge, technical or scholastic knowledge, and dynamical knowledge. Reflect on what each of these three types of knowledge means for teaching and schools.

Part 2

Seeing with New Eyes

> ***If we can shift our attention from cynicism to possibility, we can access the creative potential in all of us to imagine a better world and to participate in bringing it into being.***

Part 2 introduces the spirit of reenchantment that is so essential in our approach to work as Orientation Three teachers. Its purpose is to help develop the perceptions and sensitivities that allow Orientation Three classrooms to be successful. In fact, these perceptions lie at the heart of what this book is about. If we are to travel in a new paradigm landscape, it is necessary to be able to see the path. Seeing with new eyes means being able to recognize things that have been there the whole time but were not part of our awareness. It means being acutely aware of our new perceptions and how they are an integral part of everything we do and everything we are.

The chapters in this section emphasize joy, connectedness, wonder, and imagination. They bring forth the importance of the ordinary, of simplicity, of community. Learning and teaching are human experiences, and in these chapters, we are reconnected to the roots of our humanity. These roots enable us to confidently create new learning environments because we are able to see with purpose and clarity. These chapters show how reenchantment relates to a new kind of classroom practice.

Finally, part 2 is about possibility. If we can shift our attention from cynicism to possibility, we can access the creative potential in all of us to imagine a better world and to participate in bringing it into being.

Mythical Space

2

Terra Creare

The Landscape of Reenchantment

> ***Beware above all of crossing your arms***
> ***And assuming the sterile attitude of the spectator,***
> ***Because life is not a spectacle.***
>
> —Aime Cesairo

The landscape of ideas that comprises the world we live in today is rapidly changing. The ideas that have formed the foundation of practically every institution in our society have been found to be limited in the answers they provide for a complex world. They have taken us down a path that has led to the precipice of our own destruction. Some of us are trying to screech to a halt before we go over the cliff. Others are trying to speed ever faster, hoping that we can jump the gaping divide to the other side. There are others who want to retrace our steps and return to a time that was safer and more secure.

The ideas that have guided us down this path have been replaced gradually during the twentieth century. A new description of reality that offers a different path and a different foundation for our institutions has had an impact on virtually every discipline. We still don't understand all the implications of this alternative path, but it is more and more apparent that this new landscape of ideas will not go away. These ideas, in a strange way, take us both backward and forward. They take us back to the roots of our humanity that grounded us in the spirit of Earth and connected us to a creative and meaning-filled universe. They take us forward by giving us wings of new possibility that we have not yet realized. To walk in this new landscape, however, requires that we perceive the world in a way different from our current way. It requires us not just to think differently, but to create a new kind of living. We hope this book will help teachers live and thrive in this new landscape. We hope it will be useful in guiding them to walk a path that leads each of us to the edge of possibility.

A Place to Begin

Shifts in who we are often begin by taking a look in the mirror. We suddenly decide that things can and should be different. The three of us believe that many educators know deep inside that schools cannot remain as they are. Whether we talk to teachers, administrators, parents, or policy makers, we find that the level of frustration is very high. And yet, things remain remarkably the same after years of research, reforms, and special programs.

Teachers have told us in frustration that the nature of teaching has changed so much in the past few years that it seems almost like a different profession. The situations of our students are often heartbreaking, and teachers often feel powerless to make any real difference in the quality of students' lives. There seems to be more and more pressure to work miracles in situations where we may feel that there is less and less hope.

The problems of our age feel so complicated. It seems that any solution quickly becomes a new problem. Educators keep trying to find the source of the issue, yet when they do, it becomes intertwined with many other problems, and the cycle begins to feel insurmountable.

We hear an interesting contradiction from teachers. On one hand, teachers tell us that in many situations they "can't" do the things that they know intuitively are good for kids. It is often the administrator who won't let them or the political climate of the community or the lack of cooperation from other departments or the lack of time to plan effectively. We know that many of these are legitimate complaints. On the other hand, if we ask teachers if they are marginalized as professionals or if they are mere technicians carrying out other people's policies and expectations, they deny it and say that, when they close their classroom doors, they have quite a bit of freedom. We believe that both situations are probably true. Teachers do have a sense that they can do much more than they are doing, if there were just a little more support, freedom, and time to work more collaboratively with colleagues. Yet all of us also know that the problems in education are subsumed by the problems in society as a whole, and to approach large-scale change is impossibly daunting and overwhelming.

Education is not the only public institution that is being urged to change. All institutions that have been a major force in our lives are under attack. Look at health care, the legal system, prisons, welfare, Congress, the military, universities (which have different issues from those in education in general), business, and industry. There is a sense that each of these institutions has in its own way become misguided, ineffectual, or worse, part of the very problems it is meant to address.

In the midst of all these problems, we have lost sight of the fact that learning is natural and joyous. This book is more about a change of consciousness than it is about particular programs and innovations. Shifting our consciousness, however, is not easy. It demands giving attention to what we do and think and feel. When we apply this kind of attention to our professional lives, we begin to question many of the concepts and practices that are typical in our schools. It is not so much that they are wrong as it is that they represent a practice based on an understanding of the world that can no longer be justified. All around us our institutions are undergoing necessary, dramatic changes. Yet, how do we understand these changes and what kind of transition is necessary?

A Culture in Transition

In the midst of this institutional malaise are real people who are dedicated to making a positive difference. Teachers are doing things the way they were taught, but somehow doing a good job is no longer enough. The problems are bigger than just adding a new twist here and there. It seems that to change one thing we have to change everything!

It is like taking all the furniture in your house and piling it into the center of a room and being told to rearrange the house. Then when you are in the middle of rearranging it, being told to change everything again. Meanwhile you are living in the middle of a mess, not knowing which room is which, or what goes where. Things just don't seem to make sense.

Walker Percy suggested many years ago that the changes occurring in our culture could not yet be understood, but they could be felt. He wrote

> **The modern age began to come to an end when men discovered that they could no longer understand themselves by the theory professed by the age.**
>
> **After the end of the modern age, its anthropology was still professed for a while and the denizens of the age still believed that they believed it, but they felt otherwise and they could not understand their feelings. They were like men who live by reason during the day and at night dream bad dreams. (25)**

The situation of our time is an outgrowth of a belief system and a way of life that we, as a culture, have internalized and made real in the world. The foundation for this belief system is crumbling, both scientifically and philosophically. This breakdown will undoubtedly affect the kinds of choices we make in the future. The three of us believe that this transition represents the need for a different kind of consciousness. Willingly or not, we are all pioneers learning to inhabit a different landscape. The landscape at this point is largely perceptual but it will manifest itself in very real ways, with real consequences and real outcomes. Learning to live in this new landscape is the challenge for each and every one of us. Stephen Toulmin (1982) has said that this new kind of world "has not yet discovered how to define itself in terms of what it is, but only in terms of what it has just-now-ceased-to-be" (254).

Living in this new land may require different kinds of attitudes and skills. Yet many of the basic requirements have always been a part of us, part of the human potential that waits to be realized. Not everything that has been useful to us in the past will be helpful here. But as new skills and perceptions are created, we may find that these changes represent a range of new possibilities for each of us and the institutions that make up our lives.

Understanding Assumptions

In education as in the rest of culture, our practice is driven by assumptions about our world. Assumptions are more than just beliefs or philosophies, they represent the inner models we use to construct reality. They are a part of who we are, our beingness. It is because they are such an integral part of us that they are so difficult to be aware of, much less change. We take for granted that the world is as it seems to us. And we act as if that perception is true. For example, if we perceive content to be some "thing" to be learned, then we will approach instruction in a way that we think will best accomplish that goal. If we assume that our world is divided into objects that are basically unconnected, then we will tend to divide our curriculum into subjects, topics, and unrelated categories. Moreover, we will tend to respond to what we know in ways that suggest separateness. If we perceive the world to be comprised of causally determined and predictable actions, then our approach will focus on behavioral management and the tendency to reduce subject matter into discrete, linear units and skills. If, on the other hand, we view content as events, if we perceive the world as connected in fundamental ways, if we view action as self-generating within context and we understand process and self-organization, then our curricular and instructional decisions will be very different. It is this latter view of the world that is coming to the fore in our culture. We need an education that supports it. We need teachers who reflect it.

During the first half of this century, Alfred North Whitehead (1978) told us that the basic foundations of scientific thought required reinterpretation. It is these very foundations that our institutions and modern practices are based on. Thomas Kuhn (1962), the prominent science historian, has called this reinterpretation a "conceptual revolution." And physicist Paul Davies (1988) notes that it is like "turning three hundred years of science on its head" (22). In other words, it isn't just that new knowledge is growing, it is that this new knowledge presents a fundamentally different picture of reality than what we thought. It is natural to want to hang on to that which is familiar, to a view of the world in which our place in it is known. But this familiar world is not the world we experience. We live in a world that is characterized by an awareness of its own complexity. Simple solutions, predictable laws, and sequential steps seem less and less workable. Instead we are moving to a view of the universe where the emphasis is not on parts and elements, but rather on wholes and patterns. There is a recognition of an interrelated world where things cannot be understood in terms of separateness, but only in terms of relationship. The picture emerging is one of dynamic wholeness, of a universe in the process of creating itself. Each of us is a participant in its creation.

As a culture becomes disenchanted with the symbols and "realities" that once had value, it struggles with its own inadequacy to move beyond those beliefs. Donald Oliver (1989) suggests that as a modern people, we are bound up in a scientific-materialistic culture and live out our lives in a machine metaphor. We are unable to move past our need for a "new machine" or "new technology" to make everything all right. Yet we are increasingly disillusioned with those very technologies that make up our lives. We are unable to realize our need for more significant meaning and for a broader understanding of the relationship between our conception of technique and of deep culture.

Undoing the Machine Metaphor

Schools, like every other institution in our society, have been organized around this machine metaphor, thus operating in many ways like factories. Central to the machine metaphor are the concepts of prediction, control, and measurement. The focus of the machine metaphor is on external behavior and observable outcomes. In other words, we try to "fix" the environment, to control it according to our desires. When we do so we inevitably treat the world around us as if something is wrong with it, and in imposing our will upon it, we treat it like an object. If you have ever been treated in this way, you know it is not very pleasant. There are many kids who genuinely feel that school is a terrible place for them to be. It is not that they do not want to learn; rather, they are made to feel unworthy and out of place. Listen to some of the comments made by students in a study by Poplin and Weeres (1993) called *Voices from the Inside.*

> *In school I don't like peas, being bad, waiting in line, unfriendly people and being friendless.*
>
> —Elementary student

> *I guess the only people who understand [my problems] are gangsters. They always understand and they always help me solve it too.*
>
> —Middle school student

> *Teachers see you as a cholo, gangster, low-life, drug dealer, etc., and that makes them treat you differently than everyone else because they stereotype us and don't give us a chance to show them what we can do. Not all of us are bad, some of us want to get a good education.*
>
> —High school student

> *This place hurts my spirit!*
>
> —High school student

If the machine metaphor is an implicit assumption that operates in many of our schools, then what does it look like? Educators spend a great deal of our time and energy doing the following things: identifying problems, developing plans to attack them, establishing formal plans of action with specific outcomes, maintaining control so that those plans can be carried out, measuring the effectiveness of our intervention, and finally, developing a subsequent plan of action. The decisions about what is good or bad for someone are determined by those carrying out the interventions and the environment is organized to facilitate the "fixing" of the problems. Sound familiar? Of course it does! It is the way most of us were trained to do our jobs.

Most classrooms are not as stark as what we have described. Nevertheless, the assumptions that drive what we do are always underneath the surface. Even if we refuse to approach education in this way, we must interpret what we do in these terms.

Mary Poplin (1984) has shown that the major learning theories in use today all have mechanistic assumptions. She notes five characteristics of the most prevalent models.

1. There is a segmentation of learning. Learning is conceived of as either discrete processes, skills, strategies, or stages. Learning is therefore often objectified and separated from individuals' experience.
2. There is an emphasis on school goals rather than the life goals of individuals. Institutional interpretations dominate educational categories, labels, and possibilities.
3. All the models are deficit driven. Here, evaluation and assessment depict the learners' inadequacies and tend to label them accordingly. The individual's "pathology" is treated through a variety of remedial programs. Weaknesses and strengths are viewed as essentially separate from the total person.
4. The school selects the curricula to be learned. The curricula is too often dissociated from students' lives and their own quests for meaning and significance.
5. There is an obsession with objectivity and fact. Supposedly, there are right and wrong ways to process information. There is also an unnecessary emphasis on right answers. Right and wrong processes, and right and wrong answers drive assessment and evaluation.

If learning is an essentially natural process, are we, in fact, preventing learning from happening by the assumptions we bring to our schools?

The scientific and technical nature that embodies the machine metaphor provides an aspect of legitimacy and professionalism. It is something in which we can find some degree of security and seek to control. It is not that this model cannot be useful under various circumstances. There are some needs in education that can be approached effectively by applying these assumptions in the short run. When these assumptions dominate what we do, however, and how we structure our organizations, we may want to reconsider their benefit.

The machine metaphor no longer characterizes what we know about the nature of reality. It also does not describe what we have discovered about learning in the last fifteen years. The three of us believe that many educators are beginning to realize that what we know about learning and about the nature of effective organizations is not what is happening in most of education. The assumptions of the present system are increasingly inadequate to address the issues of our time. It is not that they are necessarily wrong; it is that mechanistic assumptions work best in more tightly controlled circumstances. Once you explore the world of complexity, mechanistic assumptions and approaches based on those assumptions will no longer work.

As a society, we have been treating the world as a machine for more than three hundred years. Descartes, the 16th century French philosopher who was so influential in the development of this philosophy, stated "I do not recognize any difference between the machines made by craftsmen and the various bodies that nature alone composes" (quoted in Capra 1982, 61). When we construct a modern culture based on these ideas, that culture loses its sense of connection with a part of itself. The world becomes data and phenomena to be used and molded to our expectations and desires. Where is a sense of relationship? Where is our connection and participation with nature? How do we describe ourselves as physical and spiritual beings? Where is the mystery, wonder, awe, and joy of belonging to a universe beyond our imagination? Reenchantment is about reclaiming and accentuating these aspects of the human experience. It is about rediscovering who we are.

A Crisis of Separation

More and more, the story of our separation from the universe and one another is being told. It is a story of a culture and a civilization that in many ways has lost touch with Earth, with one another, and with a sense of participation in the universe. It is not a new story. Most spiritual traditions throughout the world have identified separation and loss of connection as one of the major characteristics of the human condition. What is new is that this condition of separation and its consequences has entered the mainstream of our intellectual questioning. Suzi Gablik (1993) observes that our culture is experiencing a radical breakdown of meaning and purpose, which until now has always been understood as a fundamental drive of human life. She is not just talking about the kind of personal meaning we may or may not find in the process of living; she is referring more to a sense of community that allows symbols of meaning to find modes of expression. "It is the spirit, or 'binding power' holding everything together, the pattern connecting and giving significance to the whole, that is lacking in the underlying picture we have of our world" (30). If separation is a pervasive characteristic of our modern world, then it is also a part of the institutions that world has created.

The human species has not always been alienated in the ways we are today. Many indigenous cultures around the world have preserved to a great extent a view of an earlier time in our history when we lived with greater connection and participation. While we cannot reverse time or travel to an earlier time, we can begin to consider how an earlier wisdom might reinform the kind of society we create. At the very least, we can become more aware of how we got to where we are.

Morris Berman's (1981) work in the sociology of knowledge is wonderfully insightful into the crisis of our times. His words ring true in our collective gut. He describes the modern epoch, encompassing the last three hundred years, as one of "progressive disenchantment." For Berman, disenchantment is a way of thinking and relating to the world that isolates us from one another. In disenchantment there is "a rigid distinction between observer and observed. There is no ecstatic merger with nature, but rather total separation from it. Subject and object are always seen in opposition to each other" (16). In a state of disenchantment, we really don't feel a part of the world around us. We don't have a sense of belonging, but instead feel that the cosmos cares very little for us. Berman calls it "a sickness in the soul" (17).

The three of us believe this condition to be more a part of today's experience than we would like to think. It is a condition that is embedded in the fabric of our institutions, in the ways we approach problems, and in the standards that our society validates as important. We also believe that most of us, "in our collective gut," don't identify with the assumptions that make up this kind of world. It is for these people that this book is being written. We want to create a different kind of practice to help us not only reframe our picture of the world, but in the process, to learn to trust in the new creations that will emerge from our practice.

Perceiving the World as Connected

When Geoffrey and Renate first gathered the significant research on the brain that has such profound implications for the way we understand learning, the overwhelming pattern that emerged confirmed that the brain is essentially a connective organ. Its potential for connections is limitless, and when we allow the brain to function optimally, we create conditions that make those connections meaningful and purposeful. The Caines also found that the brain is not some isolated organ that operates separately from the rest of us. On the contrary, we cannot separate our emotions, intuitions, or our physical well-being from the interactions of the brain. Indeed each of us is a whole being that functions as a unified entity. As they looked carefully at the research on brain functioning, they found that, just as we cannot separate the brain from the body or the emotions or the meanings that we construct, we also cannot easily delineate our perceived experiences from the rest of our being. It is this incredible sense of connectedness that led them to entitle their book *Making Connections: Teaching and the Human Brain* (1994).

Everything they found out about the brain was consistent with the other movements in twentieth century science that Sam was investigating. The worldview that asks us to separate parts from the whole, that divides the physical self from those aspects of our nature that cannot be quantified or empirically studied, that has us perceive ourselves, our natural environment, and our institutions as a machine to be tinkered with and controlled—this worldview is increasingly inadequate for the new questions of science and the new questions facing all our institutions, not just education. Wholeness, relatedness, and connectedness are new descriptors of our universe, and they can help us frame the issues we face in new ways.

Part of our task involves new ways of seeing the same things that have always been in front of us. Sam's wife, Debbie, is a fine art photographer. After twenty years in ceramics, she decided to explore a different professional media. One day, with camera in hand, she said with some degree of frustration, "I have to learn to see things differently if I want to be good at this." Sam wasn't sure what she meant and asked her to explain. She said, "I have to learn to see the effects of light, the contrasts of shadow, the hidden possibilities of an image. In photography, image and reality are not the same. I have to learn to see the images embedded in the world around me." This story illustrates that part of our challenge is to see the connections embedded in the world around us. Once we perceive the world in an expanded way, our interaction with that world becomes different.

We have found in our work with teachers that this ability to see connections and relationships is not something that is easily taught. If we don't see something, no amount of talk will convince us that it is there. If we do see it, our response is "of course!" Reenchantment is about perceiving a connected world and living a life that reflects this relatedness. It is about experiencing the joy that feeling we are connected to the world brings and creatively incorporating this joy in our classrooms and schools.

In order to see, there has to be a willingness to look. It is through the process of looking, or examining our assumptions about the world, that perceptual change happens. It is a skill that can be developed through practice and attention.

Developing a Purposeful Practice

George Leonard once wrote about the concept of mastery as it is used in eastern cultures and in the martial arts (Leonard and Murphy 1995). He pointed out, for instance, that in India mastery is a lifelong process; it is not achieved just by learning skills, but instead must become integrated into one's whole life. The martial arts in Japan and China are not characterized by graded levels en route to mastery, as they are in the United States.

Rather, one continues a routine of practice throughout one's life to discover ever new subtleties of the art, and the art reveals ever new insights about life. "Practice" is seen as a journey toward mastery.

Winton Marsallis, the great jazz and classical trumpet player, also teaches students the importance of the attitude of practice as they enter the path of musicianship. He describes how practice is not just a preparation for performance, but it is a way to feel and relate to the music at a deep level, living the life of your art.

Writers such as Julie Cameron (1992) and Natalie Goldberg (1990) insist that it is the daily practice of writing that releases us to the creative possibilities within us. Recording the free flow of thoughts and feelings assists us in discovering openings to the creative process. These two writers suggest that when we create a practice, not only does it affect the projects we are working on, but it also spills over into the context of the other activities of our lives. Indeed, each of the persons mentioned in this section see practice as an opportunity for personal growth as well as for enhanced abilities in a particular area.

Living Our Practice

We three believe very strongly that in order to really know a new paradigm or to perceive a new view of the world, one must live the paradigm. As it becomes incorporated into our daily practice, the embedded realities take new shapes and forms, and in the process our lives become changed. Over and over again, teachers who have been through the brain-based learning process report to us that not only are their classrooms different places, but perhaps more important, they have become different persons. Their view of the world has changed forever and it permeates everything they do and is part of the essence of what they have become.

Many years ago, Sam had dinner with the distinguished thinker and writer Ashley Montague. Montague related something that Sam has never forgotten. He said, "As we think back over the years about the teachers we have had, we remember far less about what they taught us than we do about the kind of persons they were and the relationship we had with them. More than anything else, we teach who we are." Over the years, the three of us have become more concerned with who we are than with specific technical attributes of teaching. Indeed, as all of us move into this new landscape of thoughts and ideas, unless we become different persons, we will not be able to establish the kinds of technical approaches necessary for a new way of teaching. It is a process. It takes time and experience, and it benefits from the mutual support of colleagues. What is most natural may at times feel unnatural, for we have supplanted nature in more ways than we can describe. Learning is natural and it is, above all, unique.

We hope to establish a practice that makes us more aware that we live on the "edge of possibility." In our classrooms and in our lives, there are no limits except the limits we create. Malidoma Somé (1995), writing on his experience of initiation into the spirit world of an African tribe, states "In the world of my people . . . when something comes into our lives that we label as impossible, like a buffalo running into a hole one foot in diameter, or a brand-new landscape opening up right before us, an elder would interpret this way of thinking as a manifestation of our own rigidity in the face of a new idea. When we resist expansion, we foster the unreal" (254).

The three of us believe that we educators have limited our imagination of the possible. We have been tainted by the cynicism of our own experience in an institution that is only halfhearted about learning. Part of the reenchantment of learning is about opening to the possibilities of what learning really means. It is the removal of unnatural preconditions that far too often prevent the possibilities that real learning unleashes.

Becoming Orientation Three teachers requires that we perceive the world in increasingly significant ways and bring our humanness into the classroom. We have found from our research and our work in schools that teaching is tied invariably to our mental models. These mental models are made up of our philosophies, our assumptions about the nature of things, and those unexamined practices that may or may not be consistent with our real beliefs. In addition, these orientations are perceptual and operate in all areas of our lives. In other words, they represent the way we see the world. They are an integral part of who we are. No matter what methods and techniques we may use, we ultimately must confront the person using the techniques—ourselves.

Each of us has within us the power to create new answers for the future. We must first change the questions and open ourselves to the process of emergence. We can become aware that our humanness is a birthright we must rediscover. It is a birthright full of promise and of hope. Jerome Haarste raises two fundamental questions that should be at the core of all that we do: "What kind of person do you want to be?" and "What kind of world do you want to live in?" If what our students are learning does not bring them face to face with these questions, then what is our purpose as educators? To quote again from Malidoma Somé (1995), "There is no reason to live if you forget what you're here for . . . When you do not know who you are, you follow the knowledge of the wind" (253). Our purpose and our practice is to discover who we are and to make learning real in everything that we do. We believe that a key to understanding this purpose is found through experiencing a reenchantment of learning.

Practice as Process

In our book *MindShifts* (1994), we describe a group process that we have used with teachers and schools to proceed through restructuring. Our research has indicated that this process has been essential to substantive, ongoing change and to creating a community of support. Teachers, administrators, secretaries, custodians, clerks, and specialized support staff all participated in groups who raised questions about the nature of learning. They shared successes and failures, fears and frustrations, insightful books and ideas, and at times they worked together on special projects. These were not work groups; rather they were learning groups who were dedicated to the continual growth of each person and to the creation of community.

Our experience has been that real change happens from the inside out. Once we begin to shift our perceptions and our focus, we begin to make natural changes that are consistent with our understandings. These shifts do not have to be major. Sometimes they are small, subtle changes; other times they reflect more dramatic leaps. For example, some of our groups began their processes with soothing, quiet music and with some beautiful art prints. They began to notice what an important difference these elements made to their group environment, so they started using music and art in similar ways in their classrooms. Within a few months, we walked into a completely different school environment. Art was in the classrooms, the office, the teachers' lounge. Children's art was everywhere. A vitality was present that hadn't been there earlier. Music could be heard at different times of the day. Morning "sings" were begun, and parents were invited to participate. An atmosphere of calm was apparent. These teachers realized that the arts are powerful factors in creating a positive, active learning environment, and that such an environment becomes brain based when it is integrated with the natural rhythms and flows of the classroom. The significance of this example is that it emerged from the process groups and through the genuine sharing of experience. It is not that this school never had art or music before, but rather that they had not been internalized into deep meaning and understood in terms of the overall purpose of learning. After the teachers felt the significance of art experiences in their own learning groups, their perception of how the arts can be used became very different. Changes emerged naturally, almost with a sense of knowing that was beyond technical understanding.

It was maintaining the integrity and the constancy of the process that allowed changes to emerge. In this way the process groups became a kind of "practice." It was a practice of community, self-reflection, and insightful sharing. We also began to understand that a significant, ongoing practice is not necessarily directed at anything in particular, but paradoxically, something particular almost always happens or emerges. This point is really important, because if you are engaging in practice, there is almost a letting go of the notion that something must occur. Whatever happens will happen naturally and over time. A short anecdote may illustrate what we mean.

Several years ago Sam took part in a theater workshop for teachers. Each day the group participated in certain activities that involved movement, improvisation, imaging, character development, and storytelling. At the end of the week, the group was to give a performance. Although they had decided to act out three "spider tales" with music, movement, and dramatic readings, there had been very little scripting or specific rehearsal. Not having had a great deal of experience in theater performance, Sam and the others were getting more and more nervous as the time to perform got nearer. They expressed their feelings to the workshop director. What she said gave everyone pause for reflection and, after a few moments, they were completely at ease: "Don't worry. All week you have been doing the things you will do on stage. You know your roles and the sequence. Just let yourself go and feel what this week has been about. Trust in the process and the performance will take care of itself." Those words, "trust in the process," have remained with Sam and the others since that time. The director was right. The performance was a huge success, but more importantly, the performers felt the truth of her words and learned an important lesson about the nature of process. It requires us to let go of the notion that something particular must happen, and instead, with a heightened awareness, allows new learning to unfold naturally.

Trusting the process is being willing to allow the unexpected to happen. Process is natural and emerges out of our participation in situations. Practice as process means that as we engage thoughtfully in a meaningful experience, it will become a process for things to happen and events to occur that seem natural and obvious. These will occur in their own time and they will be a result of an internalized shift or insight that has become a part of who you are. It is participating in an event and letting yourself and the event unfold. It is being responsive to what is going on around you and allowing others to do the same. We practice responding to what the unfolding event requires; we release our certainty about what has to happen.

Beginning Where We Are

The necessary first step in using this book is to start from where you are. You don't have to teach a certain way or have a particular set of beliefs to begin. If you are first willing to acknowledge where you are in terms of your practice, your assumptions about the nature of schooling, about the actual beliefs that guide what you do (not necessarily your stated beliefs), and about your own sense of purpose, then you have already begun. There is a quotation in *Chop Wood and Carry Water* (Fields 1984): "only by seeing where we are rather than imagining where we would like to be can we begin the process of transforming all those things we usually consider stumbling blocks into the stepping stones they really are" (9). It is not that imagining something to be better is ineffective. The point here is that it is important to recognize as honestly as you can your current place and to accept that you are where you are. This is the only place that honest dialogue can begin—whether it is with ourselves or with others.

Reenchantment means seeing the world differently within our everyday reality. It is not a single insight that happens and then we are finished. Rather, we are constantly seeing new twists that weren't there before. Or we observe what we are doing with a more sensitized awareness. All that is required is a consistent process and a willingness to look within.

This book suggests a variety of activities that we hope will open new possibilities for you, your classroom, and your school. The activities are choices, not prescriptions. They are divided into three categories. The first category of activities is directed at you as an individual. They are meant to be reflective and personal. They allow you to develop a daily sensitivity to these ideas and to respond in personal and unique ways. The second category of activities is meant to assist groups in the process of reflection and dialogue. In the appendix, you will find a description of a group process that we have used with a number of schools. If you choose to use it, we recommend that you follow it rather specifically for a couple of weeks. Then you may wish to adapt it to particular needs of your group. We would strongly suggest that if you make changes, you honor the opportunity for each person first to be heard without interruption. This adherence can have a powerful effect on the dynamics of the group and the degree of depth that can be attained. The third category of activities is directed to the classroom. These are not prescriptive in the sense that they cannot be altered. The purpose of these activities, however, is for us to begin to observe what happens when we carry these notions over to the classroom. Whether the activities are "successful" or "unsuccessful" is not the point. They are for you to observe, consider, and reflect upon. They are another way to gain insight, perspective, and a shift in perception.

Growth Is Developmental

The three of us have found that in engaging in this process ourselves, we have had to unlearn so many of the habits and perspectives we had taken for granted. None of us is immune to the influences of mechanistic values. Even as the machine metaphor begins to decline, we find its hold so pervasive in our language and discourse that it is difficult to talk of the world in any other way. These ideas have dominated the ways we think, the questions we ask, and the answers we choose. Letting go of the machine metaphor and its hold on the way we live our lives and opening ourselves to new possibilities and perspectives are the goals of this book.

Process and Reflections

Personal

1. Each morning or evening, set aside a few minutes to make a list of the things you want to do that day. After you have made your list, pause quietly with your eyes closed. Take a deep breath and feel any tension, anxiety, or questions that make you feel uneasy or challenged. Then write a few sentences about that feeling or question. Pause quietly once again, then without thinking about it, write a response to your question addressing yourself in the third person. Just let your pen flow as if the response is in the pen and not your head.

   This exercise may feel awkward at first, but we encourage you to continue this practice for a while. Pay attention to the kinds of issues you identify, what roles they play in your identity. Also begin to notice that the answers to many of our real questions are within each of us. Continue this practice throughout the time you are reading this book.

Group

1. We recommend that you use the ordered sharing process for every activity. One person shares while everyone pays full attention. Then the person to the left of the sharer shares, and so on. Focus your ordered sharing on thoughts and questions that occurred to you as you were reading this chapter. Without trying to give answers or reach conclusions, merely share your thoughts and questions with one another. What were the most powerful ideas for you? When everyone has participated, explore as a group one or more of the issues raised.
2. As part of an open discussion, begin to look for examples of the machine metaphor in your school. It might be in the schedule, the subject matter, or the way in which instruction is delivered. It might help to use Mary Poplin's analysis of instructional strategies provided in this chapter.
3. Check your collective assumptions about words and concepts used in this chapter.
   - What do you envision when you hear the word *community*? What

does *connectedness* mean to you? What role does *relationship* play in education and schools?

- We talk about "the importance of the ordinary." How do you understand this phrase and what does it mean to you?
- We speak of *possibility*. In life and work how often do we focus on possibility rather than negativity and hopelessness? What does it mean to invoke possibility and how does it relate to reenchantment?
- We discuss the roles of respect and courtesy. How are they essential to a world governed by "the reenchantment of learning"?

4. Take a few deep breaths and relax. Close your eyes and visualize a school environment that is not based on a machine metaphor. What do you see? What is happening? What kinds of relationships are there? After a few minutes, quietly share your images, using the ordered sharing process. Some may be initially uncomfortable with sitting with others and closing eyes. Sitting quietly with eyes closed is not easy to do. There may be some giggles or nervous chatter. Work through this.

Teaching

1. Look carefully at your classroom and make note of the schedule, the seating arrangements, the degree of autonomy your students have. Are these based primarily on the delivery of knowledge or on other factors? How much depth is there in your curriculum? Is there a sense of community and belonging in your classroom? Are there areas in which you feel constrained, not allowed to follow your instincts?
2. Build into your day a brief personal story that communicates to your students something about yourself as a person. If possible, focus stories on your own learning. Make sure that the story is authentic and genuine, not forced, unrelated to their interests, or "preachy." Use your own judgment about what is age appropriate. You may also want to ask your students to share something about themselves that they feel is important.
3. Pay attention to the unexpected things that happen in the course of a day. See if you can pick up on one of these events and use it in the context of your class. Once you have established a genuinely trusting atmosphere and have an orderly community in place, you might want to give an open-ended assignment with no directions and observe their decision-making processes.
4. Notice places in the curriculum you can invoke the notions of community, connectedness, and relationship.

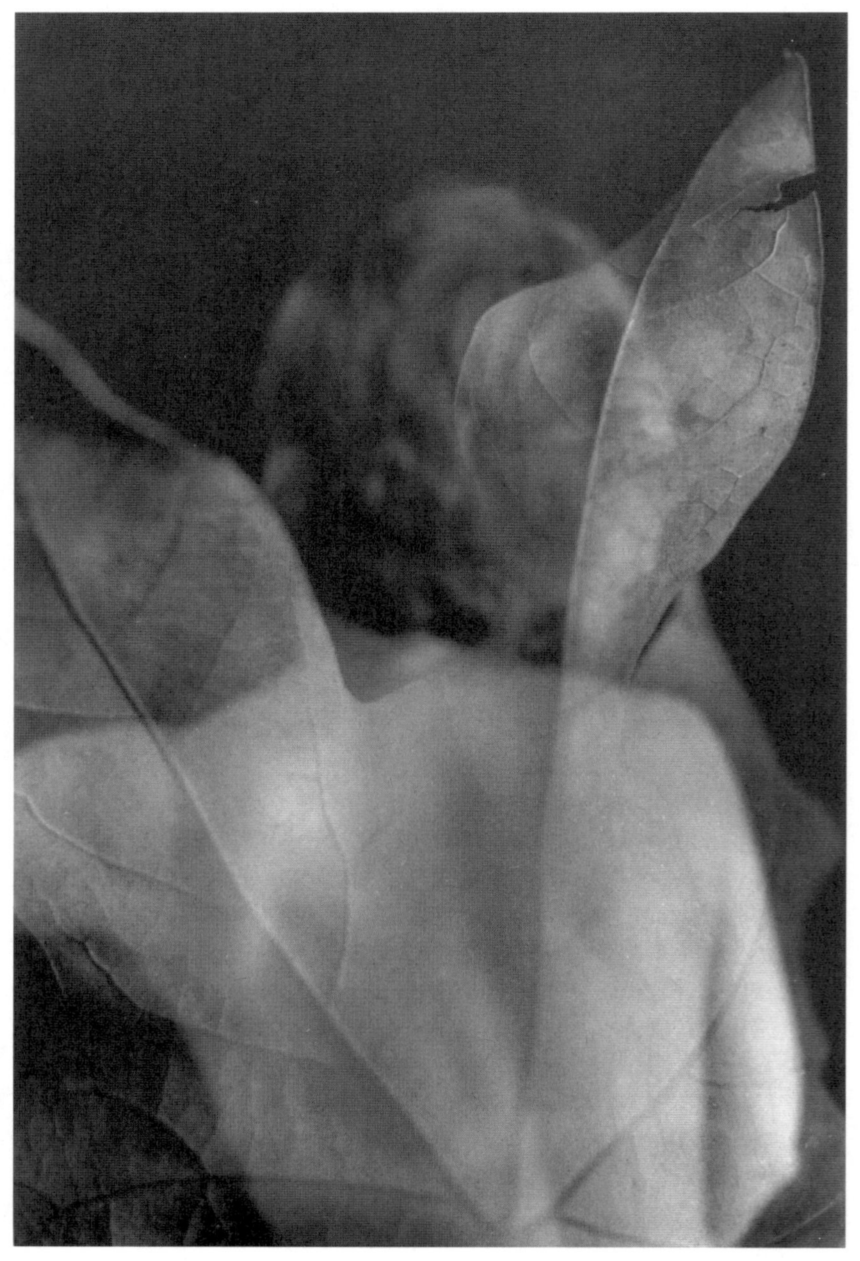

Wings

3

Reclaiming the *Joy*

The Reenchantment of Everyday Life

> *Let my joys be simple ones*
> *that know the moment for its possibilities*
> *and see in all,*
> *the smile of the universe.*
>
> —Sam Crowell

The three of us were talking with some teachers recently when several of them noted that they had lost a lot of the joy in their work. It seemed as if they had been pushing so hard to implement this or that new approach that everything had become a struggle. They were working so hard they had forgotten how to have fun along the way. As we discussed this lack of joy further, we found that many of them were having to make difficult choices between their professional and personal lives. They didn't see how they could continue at the pace they were going without burning out.

Once the joy is removed from our endeavors, the inevitable questions become, "Why am I doing this?" "What's the use?" When we lose a sense of deep contentment and joy, our lives feel lost and disconnected from anything that is important. Sometimes the result is depression, aimlessness, or just sheer escapism. We search for something that can give us the feeling of happiness or fulfillment.

Reenchantment is about viewing the world with a sense of joy. Joy is a primal feeling. It is a spark inside of us that is like an inner smile. It is a sensation of pure delight that makes us feel almost childlike. It is a magic within us that gives us total satisfaction and a feeling of completeness.

Have you ever been on a walk and stopped to observe a beautiful sunset and felt as if you were being filled up inside? Have you ever looked at the stars at night and felt overcome with a sense of awe and wonder? Have you ever touched the silky soft skin of a baby and thought about the newness of life, or watched a new plant emerge from the underworld of the soil and wondered how such an incredible thing could happen? Have you been on a trip and stopped at a scenic overlook and felt a deep sense of inspiration or sat by a beach watching the waves roll in continuous rhythm and felt the immense span of time? Have you ever experienced a feeling of being almost overcome with emotion at a musical performance or stood in front of a painting unable to move, as if captured in a trance? If any of these experiences feel familiar or remind you of other events where similar feelings occurred, you have felt the power of joy and enchantment.

Enchantment is not something that is alien to our experience; it is a natural part of life. It is not some mysterious phenomenon available only to a few; rather, it is one of those ineffable experiences that all humans have in common. It is a state of being in which we are suddenly aware of a deep sense of connection. This awareness seems to touch our very depths and evoke questions and emotions that are difficult to describe. We are in awe of the world and we have a feeling of deep gratitude.

A Culture without Joy

Modernist culture tends to use technical and scientific language to describe experience. Health is described in scientific terms. Our mental states are separated from our behaviors. We view our relationships with others often in self-interested ways or as a competitive game. We view the environment as a resource to be managed carefully, but not with a sense of interconnection. We live in a time when we are dissociated from ourselves, from others, and from the natural environment. We have come to see our problems "as an inability to discover a new piece of technical information" (Oliver 1989, 2). Our modern, technical culture has lost a sense of the relationship with those essential aspects of the world that contribute most to our humanity—the simplicity of joy, the wonder of reenchantment.

In schools, there is also a tendency to objectify the world and treat it as separate. Our curriculum is too often a world of facts and information that we present as if it were an isolated reality, as if it were separate from the students who receive the information. The focus is weighted so much on the external nature of our experience that our interior selves and our reciprocal relationship with the world go lacking. We use knowledge as a commodity to solve technical problems, reach logical conclusions, analyze complex events, and demonstrate the quantity and accuracy of our information and skills. These approaches are not wrong in themselves, but they reinforce a view of the world that is mechanistic and sterile. When the things we learn are disconnected from our lives, when they are bereft of meaning or significance, is it any wonder our students do not want to learn? Too often learning means to deny students' own humanity. Where is the innate joy of learning and the sheer excitement of becoming a new person each day of our lives?

A young man we know who had a goal of going into the medical profession had been accepted to a prestigious university. He was bright and full of potential, yet we later found out he had dropped out of college altogether. It wasn't that he couldn't do the work. Rather he quit college in order, in his words, "to reclaim my soul." These words are haunting because they imply that much of what we do in education is to strip away what is joyous, creative, and wondrous about learning, and instead make it a drudgery of terminology and analysis. Of course this story tells of only one incident, but we hear similar sentiments from many of our adult students who found their early attempts at schooling demeaning, irrelevant, and even elitist. Having returned to school on their own terms, they are less willing to accept the intimidation of the system. In fact, they are often somewhat amused, though angered, at the way their experience and accomplishments are completely ignored and dismissed. While some find a resurgence of excitement in learning, they also become aware more than ever of the hoops and hurdles involved in traditional schooling. If we treat adults like this, many of whom have had very successful lives and careers, how much more likely are we to dismiss the inner lives of younger students!

The Nature of Joy

What is it that makes us joyful? What are the kinds of activities and attitudes that create an exuberance within us, a desire to engage fully with life? How can we reclaim our joy? Joy can be an inherent part of deep, sustained engagement in powerful ideas, creative activity, and persistent skill development in an activity we enjoy. We asked several people at random how joy could be a greater aspect of their lives. Their responses were remarkably similar and showed an almost innate understanding and wisdom. In fact, many of them commented that if they would only listen to their own wisdom, they would have much more joy in their lives. Why is it that we let so many unimportant things get in the way of our own truth?

Following are some of the things those we surveyed had to say:

- *True joy comes from within. It is being grateful for what we have, reevaluating the positive aspects of our lives and getting back to the basics of who we are. It is spiritual.*
- *It is asking ourselves what we have given up that we were passionate about. Commit to doing something you love.*
- *I reclaim my joy whenever I let myself feel like a child—innocent and spontaneous. Whenever this happens, I say thank you over and over.*
- *Think of our happiest times. Take pleasure in the ordinary things that we do. Do something nice for someone else. That always gives me joy.*
- *Focus on humility so our ego can get out of the way. Then forgive ourselves for something.*
- *Get out in nature and sit quietly. Observe nature and take it in as part of yourself.*
- *Clear your mind and let thoughts flow in and out freely.*
- *Get into some kind of activity, maybe something that scares you. It usually involves getting rid of some fear. Prayer works for me.*
- *One of the most important things is to share. Go out and give of yourself. We often get self-centered. We need to reach out to someone else.*
- *Completely surrender. Let go of judgment and control. Be in the present moment. Get out in nature.*

Whatever the specific suggestion, in each of these comments joy involves reconnecting with ourselves, with nature, or with others in some significant way. It is the simplicity of it that is so apparent. It is the idea that we are meant to be connected, to create more connections, and to honor these as gifts for which to be grateful. In *A Simpler Way,* Margaret Wheatley and Myron Kellner-Rogers (1996) suggest that joy is part of a self-creating process: "Why is life engaged in self-creation? What are we observing when we see self-reference, when we see life taking new forms, playing with its freedom to be? We are observing that all life begins with consciousness. A self creating itself is consciousness made visible. A self referencing itself is consciousness in motion" (54). For Wheatley and Kellner-Rogers, joy is connecting to a creative universe and participating as creative beings and organizations. It is part of our biological and natural heritage. To deny that heritage is to deny part of who we are as human beings.

The recognition that the possibility of joy is inside us and is not dependent on a particular set of circumstances is liberating. It tells us that we are free to live in that space whenever we want. Joy can be a part of our everyday reality and can infuse the activities that make up our lives. There is a story about comedian Jack Benny that shows why so many people were warmed by his presence. He was always experiencing things with a sense of elation. He would come in to an important meeting where everyone was serious and tense and announce, "I just had the best milk shake ever!" Or he would call a friend when he was on the road just to say that the towels in the hotel were the softest he had ever had! The little things in life had significance for him. In a way, joy returns us when we are in a state of innocence.

Rene Dubos (1971), the distinguished microbiologist and Pulitzer Prize–winning author, wrote a wonderful book on the subject of enthusiasm. In it, Dubos notes that the word *enthusiasm* comes from the Greek *en theos,* meaning "the god within." For Dubos, as for Wheatley and Kellner-Rogers, self-creation is not just an idea but one of the realities of the physical universe. Enthusiasm is the letting out of an inner part of ourselves, permitting us to create with purpose and affirmation. Related to this concept is joy. To enjoy is to "live in joy." It is to approach the everyday circumstances of our lives with gratitude and offer an inner response that is genuine and authentic. Gratitude creates an openness to the world. To live joyfully is to be able to tap "the god within," to be able to see that simple experiences have significant possibilities. To live on the edge of possibility is to see the potential in ordinary experiences.

One who understood these concepts intuitively was Johannes Itten (1975), an art educator who gained an international reputation as a teacher. He wrote that "teaching with enthusiasm is the opposite of a preconceived, merely methodical approach . . . A teacher who communicates to his students nothing but the syllabus laid down by the authorities, using methods he learnt at the teachers' training college, can be compared to a dispenser of pills made up according to prescription, who can never be a true physician" (6). He speaks of the creative teacher as one who has a feel for the "intonation, the rhythm, the sequence of words, time, and place, the intellectual condition of the students, and all the other circumstances which create a dynamic atmosphere which cannot be recreated" (6). Itten understood that the most precious moments teachers experience are those when learning goes beyond knowing and affects the innermost being of a person.

Joyful Teaching

Sometimes teachers ask us what joy has to do with good teaching. If we base our response on the mechanistic model, we might be hard pressed to give an answer, for the mechanistic model wants us to reply in terms of measurable and quantifiable steps or with specific guidelines of what to do or not to do. Such steps and guidelines are not the way of the new paradigm landscape, however. There simply are no solutions that work in all situations. Rather than relying solely on specific techniques, we encourage teachers to understand deeply the nature of learning and to create techniques that augment their expressive vision. In the landscape of this new paradigm, we are more concerned with being able to access self-creativity than we are a particular kind of technique. We have found that the notion of self-efficacy, or the ability to trust in oneself and one's community to create workable solutions, is a distinctive feature of Orientation Three teachers. These teachers are able to draw upon the simplicity of joy and to see possibilities in ordinary experiences. If we cannot do so, it will be difficult to engage in more sophisticated skills that require being able to perceive with sufficient depth and creativity.

Orientation Three teachers seem to have an ability to capture and engage in spontaneity—their own and that of their students. Their classrooms are literally alive with creation. Information, projects, ideas, skill processes, and purposeful interaction fill the atmosphere. There is only the occasional need to hold students' attention, because the students are fully engaged in their own focused learning. In this kind of environment, the teacher is busy questioning, clarifying, consolidating, and extending what is being done. At times the teacher gives a presentation or organizes group work around specific activities. At other times, attention is focused on content, skills, and processes that are expected outcomes. But always the sanctity of the learner is preserved. There is an indefinable quality in these classrooms that emanates infectious energy. Part of that energy is joy. Such teachers do not find it unnerving that students are going in a variety of directions. Rather, they have the ability to see the possibilities within the activity and within the student. Their teaching is more than facilitating; it is a dialogue of invitation and sharing that allows the inner person to emerge. Clearly, the task ahead of us is to "become" a kind of person who is able to see the complexities of this kind of dynamism and interject ourselves, our creativity, and our students into an atmosphere of engaged learning. At the heart of this seemingly complex set of interactions is simplicity and joy.

Reenchantment is a joyful response to the world because we feel connected to it. A "joyful response" doesn't mean we are giddy or unaware of the serious problems that confront us. On the contrary, it is when we feel connected to ourselves, to others, to Mother Earth, and to the cosmos that we can look problems in the face without running away from them or allowing them to control our response to life. Reenchantment builds upon an innate joy and participation in life. Once we can concentrate our awareness on recognizing that a joyful and creative response to life is always available and make it a part of our practice, our perception of the world begins to shift. We begin to observe that we are connected at all times to a reality beyond ourselves and our situation. We begin to realize more acutely that the essence of learning and being is not dependent on an external condition, but rather comes from within us and from within our students. The focus of teaching and learning suddenly shifts because the reality we create is different from that moment on. The words of Lao-Tse illustrate this well:

Thirty spokes meet in the hub,
but the empty space between them is
the essence of the wheel.
Pots are formed from clay,
but the empty space within it is
the essence of the pot.
Walls with windows and doors form the house,
but the empty space within it is
the essence of the house.

The new sciences of this century have made it clear that at the heart of all physical matter, inner and outer reflect each other. The infinitesimal is an expression of the infinite and vice versa. If we focus only on external changes, as the mechanistic model emphasizes, change will be minimal and insubstantial. If we focus only on inner changes and do not allow them to become manifested in real life, then we will be living a contradiction. While the "space within" is the essence of real change, we also need the spokes, and the pot, and the walls with windows and doors in order to be whole.

Several years ago we were helping Dry Creek School in Sacramento, California, engage in a school transformation project. As inner changes in the teachers became more apparent, we recognized a reluctance to change, as well. Even when something is not working, we want to hold on to what is comfortable. So we asked a professional clown to come in and help the school experience what it feels like to risk within an environment of support. Teachers, administrators, and staff let go of their inhibitions and "became" clowns. You should have heard the laughter, felt the enthusiasm, and sensed the energy that was created. It wasn't necessarily easy, but it was actually fun to shed the shackles of old comfort zones. We processed the experience in terms of the joy of being spontaneous, taking risks, and being playful. This process was a prelude to asking teachers to try some innovative ideas and to be more spontaneous in the classroom. Even five years later, some teachers comment on the significance of that experience.

As we shift in our perceptions of the world and begin to see it in new terms, it is important to explore the implications in creative and expressive ways, and to allow our students to do the same. Johannes Itten (1975) suggests that "imagination and creative ability must first of all be liberated and strengthened. If new ideas [and perceptions] are to assume artistic form, physical, sensual, spiritual, and intellectual forces and abilities must all be equally available and act in concert" (8). Once we give ourselves permission to engage in joyful teaching, our imagination opens up more and more because we begin to see the possibilities all around us. The same thing happens when we give these opportunities to our students. Joy comes from within and from sensing our connection to a creative universe.

The Simplicity of Everyday Life

Many of us feel threatened when someone suggests that we take a creative and joyful approach to teaching. Either we feel that such an approach will not be supported by administrators and parents, or we feel that we just are not creative persons. First, there is a misconception that creativity is something that is unconventional or far out. Sometimes it is, but far more often it is in the realm of the ordinary. It is not the object we create that brings joy; rather it is the creative response. It is the act of creativity that is self-affirming. Second, creativity does not mean starting from scratch and reinventing the wheel. It is being aware that there are always more possibilities than are obvious. When we are open to exploring these possibilities just to see where they lead us, we are making a creative response to the situation. We do it all the time. Certainly, you do it more than you think in your teaching and also in your life outside the classroom. For example, consider the times you made adjustments to a recipe or made new decisions at the last minute or planned a special party for someone's birthday. The point we hope to make is that just the very practice of being aware that there are always more possibilities than are obvious helps to make those possibilities visible.

Geoffrey constantly uses the phrase "And there's more . . . " Whatever we choose to do, whether doing a completely self-designed activity or following the instructions in a teacher's guide, there are always a multitude of other choices that we could make. Why did we choose the one we did? Was it something that was joyful to be a part of for us and for our students? Did it help us feel connected in some way to the significance of what may have been learned? Were we or our students able to meaningfully explore other possibilities? The reality of "and there's more . . . " is always a part of everything we do. Every act of living is laden with possibility. If there is a trick to encouraging creativity, it is to focus our attention on creating an environment and experiences in which students can be expressive and engaged, and can explore multiple possibilities. This focus helps us remember why we are in the classroom in the first place.

Focusing on learning that is joyful and participative helps us make the right kinds of choices. When we make choices, it is important to be aware of the other choices we did not make and the vast possibilities that are always available. Equally important is to become aware of ourselves as we select our choices. Duane Elgin (1993) writes that we must be conscious of both the choices and the chooser if we are to transform our living. If we are continually making decisions that reflect socially and psychologically conditioned patterns, then what do our choices say about the assumptions that drive what we do? "The more conscious we are of our passage through life, the more skillfully we can act and the more harmonious can be the relationship between our inner experience and our outer expression" (126). Even if we spout a philosophical litany that we think we believe, if our choices are really governed by other habits and patterns, then it is those that comprise our mental models. It is amazing to notice how many of our activities are taken for granted as part of our identity, when in reality they have merely slipped into our living with little or no conscious thought. Elgin elaborates on our almost constant state of mental distraction:

> **Consequently, by virtue of a largely unconscious social agreement about the nature of our inner thought processes, we live individually and collectively almost totally embedded within our mentally constructed reality. We are so busy creating ever more appealing images or social facades for others to see, and so distracted from the simplicity of our spontaneously arising self, that we do not truly encounter either ourselves or one another. In the process we lose a large measure of our innate capacity for voluntary, deliberate, intentional action. (127)**

Becoming consciously aware of the simple activities of our everyday lives and what patterns drive those actions is a key to opening our capacity for genuine joy. For when we become aware of automated patterns that are not consciously intended, then we are no longer bound by them. They may continue for a while until we know what to replace them with, but they do not have a hold over us. Do not suppose that developing such awareness is easy. On the contrary, it is a life's work. To the extent that we can move toward this heightened awareness, however, we feel liberated and we feel the joy of our human capacity.

Being Aware of the Ordinary

There is a phrase the three of us have heard that says "the sacred is in the ordinary." It is meant to convey that while bursts of insight and epiphanies are not to be denied, it is the path we walk each day that is most significant. We believe that this phrase also applies to our educational practice. Becoming acutely aware of the ordinary leads us to see the potential of each moment. This ability is not some magical ability; it is within the grasp of each of us. This kind of awareness is part of that quality called *with-it-ness*. The term refers to that ability to be aware of what is happening at the moment it is happening and being able to respond in the appropriate way. It isn't something you can teach, but it can be developed, sometimes through coaching, but mostly by reflection. To develop this quality one must learn to be aware of those ordinary events that occur and see beyond them. It might be that look of frustration on a child's face or the tone behind an impertinent response that belies fear or insecurity. It might be sensing when a transition must take place or when to go off on a tangent in response to student interest. Whatever forms it might take, "with-it-ness" is a kind of awareness that allows us to make spur-of-the-moment decisions or to draw attention to something that is taking place in the classroom.

If you have ever watched a master teacher at work, you may have marveled to yourself, "How did she know to do that?" or "Wow! I would have never thought of going in that direction with this subject matter." Developing a sense of awareness and an understanding of things beneath the surface provides the teacher with the resources to greatly expand instructional and curriculum possibilities. Those resources are not external and do not have to be purchased; they lie within each one of us. At first, there is a tendency to want to break all the behaviors into small parts and then learn each of those elements separately as a set of cumulative techniques. Certainly educational research has worked hard to do that very thing. And yes, sometimes it is helpful. We can coach, give feedback, explain reasons, and give hints. But what cannot be taught is the awareness and the timing and the intuitive understanding of what needs to happen. It is like a noncomedian trying to do a comedy routine he saw on television without having a sense of timing or the delivery that makes the jokes successful.

A student teacher once tried to mimic his master teacher's method of dealing with a student disturbance. The young man walked over until he was very close, made stern eye contact, and waited. Then he returned to the front to continue his presentation. About every few moments he repeated this "technique" in a different part of the classroom, each time totally interrupting what he was doing. The poor young man looked so ridiculous the class almost burst out laughing. He had absolutely no idea how to implement the technique. We see similar things happening over and over again throughout education, although in less dramatic ways. We see teachers claiming to teach whole language who end up not teaching anything at all. Real whole language can be tremendously successful, but it is philosophically and perceptually based; it is not a set of procedures or techniques. Without a depth of understanding it is often misused. We see technology programs that are called that only because technology is available. We see group work that is more of a seating arrangement than an approach to good teaching. Yes, techniques can help. Yet to make a difference, they must be accompanied by a deep sense of awareness and intuitive understanding of complex dynamics and the overall purpose of learning. As this book explores the reenchantment of learning, keep in mind that there is no particular technique required. Reenchantment is a place where our knowing and our being merge.

We had been working in a school with teachers who were interested in connecting the required curriculum to larger, more global themes. They had been trying to go beyond what they were asked to teach as well as to help students develop specific skills and knowledge of content that related to standardized tests and evaluations. They saw each goal as a separate kind of activity that required different kinds of planning, different materials, and different teaching styles. They complained that there just wasn't enough time in the day to do all the things that one thinks one should do. How could they add more to what they were teaching and develop new ways of effectively helping their students learn? We did some demonstrations by taking their current curriculum and finding natural global themes that enhanced what they were teaching, and we also showed how they could embed narrow, specific skills just as easily—without a different "lesson plan" and without a huge investment in time and resources. When we were finished, one of the teachers commented, "I get it. You don't have to create the global connections; instead you have to learn to see them, to be aware of them. The connections are always there. Once we learn to recognize them, they almost fall into place." Becoming aware of the ordinary is developing the ability to see with different eyes. It is being able to recognize the possibilities that are right in front of us.

The brain responds readily to the process of finding new patterns and seeing relationships. This process is not only enlightening, it is enjoyable. When we begin to play with our ability to find connections and to see beyond and within the ordinary, we discover that the ordinary is a brand new world of promise and possibility. This ability is within each one of us. As a Chinese proverb states,

Know the truth
Without leaving your doorstep.
See its face
Reflected in the window.
To seek it outside
Is to leave it behind.

We have been so conditioned to look at isolated fragments of knowledge that the only way we know to go deeper is to add more on. For example, state skills tests seem to imply that each skill requires a separate objective and an isolated lesson. Teachers who try to address all the demands for teaching students skills and content often feel that the task is overwhelming and unrealistic. If teaching them these skills in this way seems impossible that's because it is. The additive approach to teaching and learning will only go so far, then something has to give. When each of the additions has to have an objective of its own, teachers can be responsible only for a limited number of additions. Do we really think that our own personal knowledge is the sum total of the objectives that someone has taught us? If not, then why do we impose such an absurd restriction upon ourselves?

Education, by continuing to define itself in these narrow terms, falls into the trap of having to depersonalize the learner, the teacher, and the school. It is a mindset that must ultimately fail. The problems are tied to a set of assumptions that greatly restrict us. Applying the mechanistic model to education, we have become strangers to ourselves. Our curriculum has been sterilized and broken apart into meaningless pieces. Our instruction has been separated from those who instruct. The teacher has been made a technician without a voice of her own. The student has been seen as something to be manipulated and controlled, with nothing to give, little to say. It is necessary now to go beyond these assumptions and the education it spawned. It is time to reconnect to the world we are trying to learn about and to become different kinds of participants in that world.

There Is More Than What We See

We are not going to find a quick fix to our problems or create some magical technical or social solution. There is not some wonder drug that is going to make everything all right. Instead, the three of us believe that we as educators must connect more deeply to our own humanity and come to understand, in the words of Joseph Campbell, that "outer and inner space are the same" (28). Quantum science tells us that we live in a world of connection and wholeness. It is a world where external and internal experiences are equal participants in the reality we know. This is the place of enchantment, that place where we are part of the unfolding of a creative universe. Chemist Donald Andrews (1966) asks us, "Will we look down and see only the sterile dust of mechanistic atoms beneath our feet, or will we look up and see beyond the starry sky the prismatic reaches of infinity? Will we retain in our mind the impenetrable darkness of ignorance; or will we open our heart to the rainbows of the unseen and to the harmonies of the unheard so that the strange beauty of the world will be like madness in our blood?" (421). Andrews describes a mental place where joy feeds our soul. It is the place where enchantment begins. It is all around us in everyday life.

Science tells us that we are only able to see and hear less than a millionth part of all the light and sound that occurs in our everyday lives. What we consider reality is made up of a very limited sensory range. Most of reality lies beyond our physical senses. In other words, most of what is real is invisible and inaudible to us. Consider the following description by Donald Andrews (1966) of the light and sound happening right now if our sight and hearing could perceive it. Pretend for a few moments that you can.

> **Now look around you. The room is ablaze with dazzling light. The chairs, the tables, the floor, the ceiling, and the walls are prismatic crystals, sparkling with a thousand shades of red, yellow, green, and blue such as you have never in your life seen before. Your clothes are on fire with a million microscopic rainbow flames. Your nose, your cheeks, your hands are shining ruby, emerald, and sapphire. You open your mouth and a shaft of amethyst light beams out before you. The air itself sparkles as if millions of miniature meteors are darting all around you, as if a cluster of skyrockets had just exploded. There is a swift rain of tiny incandescent bullets shooting down from the ceiling, shooting through the table, through the chairs, right through your body, and disappearing into the floor.**
>
> **Almost blinded by this strange blaze of light, you shut your eyes in bewilderment. Suddenly you are aware of a hurricane of sound beating upon you, as if a thousand symphony orchestras were magically squeezed into the room and all playing fortissimo. For every object near you is resonating with its own strange, peculiar music. The table booms like a hundred big bass fiddles doing a bolero. The lamp is trilling like a dozen flutes. The carpet is caroling. In this very book you hold in your hand, you hear a chorus of a thousand voices. And your body is vibrant with the**

> **most complex music of all. You hear a super-symphony resounding within you—melody, harmony, counterpoint—canon and fugue intermingling in a tapestry of sound with tones millions of times more varied, with texture millions of times more complex than any symphony ever dreamed of by a human composer. (15–16)**

Andrews's description is not science fiction. It is real in the same way as the table and chairs we can see are real, in the same way as our favorite song we can listen to is real. And even this description is only a small part of the reality beyond our senses. If we can begin to have a feeling for the reality that we cannot see or hear, and understand that there is more than meets the eye to everything, then we can be open to the notion of "And there's more . . . " When we realize that beneath every tangible object and every fragment of content information there is a world beyond our wildest imagination, then reenchantment comes nearer to being a reality. We are ready to explore the infinite layers of meaning that make up the ordinary world of events and life.

The Personal Nature of Learning

When we view learning as merely the regurgitation of content or see it as mass production of specified curriculum outcomes, we risk depersonalizing not only the content but our students, as well. Just because we may make allowances for different ways of learning, if we have not engaged the individual stories and perspectives, the unique questions and interests of our students, then we are still a long way from personalizing the learning process.

Several years ago a very bright student teacher was having difficulty reaching his class. The young man was extremely talented, spoke several languages, had studied at Oxford, and spent several years in the work force. He approached the class with great enthusiasm, endless hours of preparation, and much creativity. He reached a high level of frustration, however, during the teaching of a unit on Greek civilization, one of his favorite subjects. His sixth-grade students seemed totally disinterested, confused, and disruptive. At first he thought it was his discipline techniques and he decided to clamp down. His students became quieter and less disruptive, but they were not learning any better. Then he thought he might be "over their heads," so he decided to make the content simpler. His new approach made very little difference. He made other changes, but to no avail. How could a subject he knew so much about and loved so much be so boring to his students? What was wrong with them? In a flash of insight the young teacher suddenly realized that it was he who owned the love of Greek civilization, not his students. He had researched the time period, studied the major personalities, learned the language, read the epics, traveled personally to the country, and visited the sites. He had nurtured this interest and love over years and now he was trying to "rent" his love of Greece to his students. He realized that they would have to develop their own love and interest for the topic for it to mean anything to them.

It was an insight that changed everything for this young teacher. Almost immediately he started sharing his own story about his fascination with Greek civilization. Students joined in with their stories. Questions were raised, projects were formed, and an entire array of ideas came from the students. What had been a dismal failure turned into an overnight success. The teacher went on to become one of the most creative and effective teachers at the school. He had learned that learning has to be personal if it is to make a difference. When students have a personal interest and investment in what they are learning there will be a qualitative difference in their performance and attitude. The excitement of learning glows in their eyes and in their hearts.

When students have a personal interest and investment in what they are learning there will be a qualitative difference in their performance and attitude.

The change in this teacher's approach was part of his change of perspective. It wasn't that any one technique was particularly brilliant or effective, but everything in the class began to reflect his new perception. The way he interacted with the students, the way discipline was handled, the way curriculum was approached all became different because he was different. He no longer viewed what he was doing in the same way. Although this teacher continued to learn technical aspects of teaching, he had transformed his thinking about what it means to teach. He personalized his own experience of teaching and everything seemed to change at once.

Learning becomes personal when we allow it to have meaning for individual students and when we relate that meaning to a sense of purpose and connectedness. When we stop separating learning from the human experience and instead begin to see how learning can become a threshold to the broader themes of life itself, we enter the realm of reenchantment. Reenchantment is not a recipe of new approaches; rather it is a different way of viewing the world and what we do.

As you move into the subsequent chapters of this book, you will find it helpful to understand that this is a living curriculum. It is approaching life and our teaching with an affirmation of self-creation and awareness, of perceiving ever new possibilities, and of realizing that we are part of a connected and whole universe.

To Nature

M*y every move is your dance*
and the words from my mouth, your music.
I sing unrestrained for joy and gladness
and paint your canvas with my eyes.
Your landscape is my stage
where dramas and comedies and tragedies
are played out—
And still I sing
and dance
and join together the colors
you hold before me.

I *write words that cannot describe you,*
tiny scratch marks on paper
that are whispered in my ear.
I walk in your presence,
undone by your glory—
in awe of you.
I do not understand our connection,
but I know I am part of you.
I look beyond in the darkness
only to see you in the light of the stars.

You are above me and below.
I taste the nectar
of the wind.
I turn in all directions
and find you,
and I sleep under the crescent moon.

Dance with me and sing your song.
Be my lover and receive me
inside your heart.
Take me beyond the boundaries
of life's canvas,
beyond the temporal limits
of a single event.
Participate in my play of life,
and write your words that transcend my knowing.

I lie silent in your sweet grasses
of refuge,
looking into clouds,
listening to murmuring brooks
splash over stones and rocks
singing for joy.

—Sam Crowell

Process and Reflections

Personal

1. Continue the activity you began in the previous chapter of making your daily list and being aware of your feelings about the day. Identify an issue or question and respond spontaneously in the third person.
2. Spend a few moments alone somewhere outside where there is natural growth of trees or plants. Just take in the colors, the shapes, the smells. Look at the sky and feel the breeze. Absorb the sun and notice the contrasts of shadows. Touch the bark of a tree and the greenery of the plants. Notice how many things that we so often take for granted are full of texture and fullness. Say quietly to yourself, "I am profoundly aware of and grateful for the presence of these things in my life." Repeat this statement for several days.
3. Do something just for fun that you have been wanting to do for a while. Plan it ahead of time and make it a special event just for you. Enjoy without guilt. After your special time, reflect on the feeling of joy the experience evoked and what it means. What is it inside of you that happened? How does this experience relate to the rest of your life? Is there room for these types of experiences in the world of someone who is responsible and sensible?
4. Write a short poem or description about a simple, ordinary event that brings you joy.

Group

1. Using ordered sharing, share experiences you engaged in this week that heightened your awareness of the ordinary and made you more conscious of simple joy.
2. Give yourselves some time to go back over this chapter. What ideas, words, or concepts do you want to discuss? Remember that we ultimately want to "live" these ideas in our own lives, which is different or goes beyond simply enjoying the ideas. For example, "trusting in our community" sounds wonderful. But what is that trust made of? How is it strengthened?
3. How are you as a group dealing with conflict and conflicting views? Dealing effectively and respectfully with blind spots, strong emotions, and opinions is important in creating a trusting and supportive community. Is "working through" difficulties and problems part of the ordinary that we can also celebrate? Can someone in the group

recommend a book or teach a conflict resolution process? How are these questions related to the notion of reconnecting and joy? Process? Learning?

4. An idea discussed in this chapter is moving from focusing on the negative or what isn't working or can't work to the possibilities and potential that exists in every situation. Catching our own fascination with the *no* and the negative is hard work. See if you can spot a few of these negatives either as a larger community, in your dialogue as a group, or in personal examples. Turn these into positives. Identify the learning or potential in the examples you give. What are the possibilities?

   How do we help one another change focus from tragedy to possibility on a more or less regular basis?

5. Generate a list, similar to the one shared in the section The Nature of Joy near the beginning of this chapter, that answers the questions "What is it that makes us joyful?" and "How can we reclaim our joy?" Discuss among yourselves the significance of your lists.

Process Check

Have you developed a way of opening and closing your group session? If at all possible, the opening and closing should not include talking. One example might be opening or closing your activities with some soft music and quiet reflection. The opening and closing can be as simple as taking one deep breath together and exhaling slowly. Ultimately they can be anything you agree on as a group, as long as it marks an observed and comfortable way to signal a beginning and end.

Teaching

1. Pause deliberately several times throughout the day and quietly observe what is happening. Find something that you can take joy in and privately treasure it.
2. Share with your students something about a subject area they are studying that genuinely excites you. Be spontaneous and perhaps share a personal experience that made you love that particular subject. It is important to be honest and not fake it.

   Allow for informal comments if they have any.

3. Do something out of the ordinary with your students just for the fun of it. Later, reflect on the experience.
4. Identify a traditional pattern you have used over the years but that no longer serves you or the students. What are the possibilities for doing what this pattern is meant to do in a new and better way? Do you feel free to discuss new possibilities with your students?

Seeds of Rebirth

4

Reenchantment as a *Sense of Connection*

> *When we try to pick out anything by itself, we find it hitched to everything else in the universe.*
>
> —John Muir

Why is connectedness so important to humans? Whether it is the need to belong or be accepted, or whether it is the desire to be a part of something larger than ourselves, humans seek out some reassurance that we are not alone, not isolated from the rest of creation. Connectedness is more than just a need, however; it is a reality. Perhaps nothing else better describes the central motif of reenchantment than connectedness. The teacher who is successful in the land of reenchantment is the one who sees, and feels, and lives a sense of connectedness. Having a sense of connection is so central to living in this new landscape that without it, we are only going through the motions. It is the key to a new understanding of learning, to a substantive change in our curriculum, and to a new kind of relationship with our students. The voices of the new sciences point out repeatedly that we live in a relational world. For us, however, the argument for connectedness is less important than the reality of it as we incorporate it into our living and being. The more we can see and feel connectedness, the more it can be integrated into what we do in the classroom and who we are as teachers.

Can We "See" Connectedness?

Connectedness is both obvious in its simplicity and subtle in its complexity. For example, imagine holding a small leaf in the palm of your hand. It may feel cool to the touch. It may be soft or brittle. It may drape along the outside boundaries of your fingertips or fit snugly in the curvature of your hand. Imagine what you see. Do you see the variation of color? Do you notice the veins that support its structure and carry within them the nutrients of life? Do you notice size and shape, or find yourself associating the leaf with a category of *tree*? These kinds of observations are normal, yet they describe only a detached relationship with the leaf, not necessarily a connected one. Our senses provide us with information that allows us to describe or explain what we perceive. Even if we enhanced our powers of perception by using microscopes and other instruments, we would only have a more detailed account of something separate and removed from us. So what does connectedness look like? Is it possible to learn to "see" it? In order to have a sense of connectedness in our lives, it is necessary to perceive it in the world. What does that mean?

Imagine that as you hold the leaf in the hollow of your hand, you reflect on the way you both breathe life into each other—the leaf, giving you oxygen, and you, giving it carbon dioxide. Just like you, it lives among many of its kind. It is connected to a group of other leaves that connect to branches and more branches and finally to a tree. We have similar kinds of connections in our own lives—families, communities, nations, and planet. Can you see that the leaf's surface functions much like our own skin and that its veins work in a way similar to ours? The leaf is an integral part of our conception of color and part of our understanding of spring, summer, and autumn. If the leaf could talk to you, what do you think it would tell you about its life? What would you tell it about yours? As you imagine holding the leaf in your hand, visualize that at the subatomic level it is literally a part of your hand and that you are literally a part of it. You both manifest in different ways the energy of the sun and the essence of life and creation. In this reflective exercise, are you able to see beyond the original description of the leaf to a more intimate, shared experience of life? Can you perceive the outline of connectedness? In this chapter we will examine what connectedness means from many points of view and begin to explore the implications it has for us as individuals and teachers, for classroom communities, for our curriculum, and for our schools as organizations.

We Are Part of a Bigger Picture

There is a story about an African tribe in which each person is given a unique song. The songs start before they are born. The prospective mother leaves the village to commune deeply with nature, declaring her desire to conceive a child. She feels herself a part of nature and sees her bringing life into the world as a sacred act. She asks to participate in the creative process of nature. During this time of solitude, she waits until the song of her unborn child is given to her. It is a unique song never sung before. She learns the song and departs home to teach the song to her husband before they attempt to conceive. After she becomes pregnant, the woman gathers around her the midwives and teaches them the song, and they in turn teach the song to others in the village. When the child is being born, the midwives sing the child's song as his or her introduction to the world. At each special occasion in the growing child's life, the song is sung. The song is meant to connect the person to a unique place in nature, to family, and to village. Throughout the person's life, the song announces uniqueness and connectedness. When death finally comes, the song is sung for the last time.

The significance of this simple act is the profound realization that we are all unique beings on this Earth and that we also are connected unalterably to our Earth community and to that which is beyond our knowing. When we view the classroom as a participating and living community that supports the individuality of each person and creates a common bond of our togetherness, we can begin to ask the kinds of questions that lead to a different emphasis, atmosphere, and approach to learning. Beyond this sense of our connectedness in community are other important aspects of what it means to be connected. If we were to set only one question before you as a human being or as a teacher, it would be "What does it mean to be connected to everything—all reality?"

Over the years of human history, our society has somehow lost a sense of this integrative spirit. And recently in our history, this isolation from our essential nature has resulted in a pathology we call "the modern age." Thomas Berry (1990) writes that "for too long we have been away somewhere, entranced with our industrial world of wires and wheels, concrete and steel, and our unending highways, where we race back and forth in continual frenzy" (1). Those who analyze the larger culture suggest that this lack of connection has had devastating consequences—"The death of the spirit, the amputation of the soul, the sense that all our gods are dead: these are the messages we have been programmed to give and receive by our culture, which works by legitimizing certain ways of knowing and disqualifying others" (Gablik 1993, 46). By breaking things up into isolated fragments and putting undo emphasis on reducing things to their smallest components, by treating human experience as cumulative aspects of observable behavior and seeking to engineer results and outcomes, we have unwittingly removed meaning and connectedness from our cultural discussion.

That the institutions created by such a culture reflect those perspectives is not surprising. The reenchantment of learning, thus, is not just a pathway to a different kind of teaching; it is a cultural project to infuse meaning, significance, and community into our lives. As physicist David Bohm states, "To call for nonseparation, is of course, to ask for a tremendous revolution in our whole attitude toward knowledge. But such a change is now necessary and indeed long overdue" (in Griffin 1990, 68). Reenchantment requires a sense of connectedness.

What Does Connectedness Really Mean?

One of the schools we work with has created banners in each of the classrooms that read "Everything is connected." The teachers, administrators, support staff, and students have a sense that they are all important elements of the total community and that they are part of an organization that is interdependent. There is also some sense that every subject is somehow embedded in every other subject, and that beyond all subjects is the reality that subjects themselves are merely arbitrary separations of a world and universe that is essentially whole. These are vague understandings, yet they provide a kind of focus to explore continuously what connectedness really means in the nuts and bolts of everyday life. We ask these teachers to confront the constant question, "If everything is connected, what does that mean in this situation or that situation, or in terms of our curriculum, or the way we teach? What is the nature of connectedness?"

Physicist Fritjoff Capra (1982) writes that "the conception of the universe as an interconnected web of relations is one of two major themes that recur throughout modern physics. The other theme is the realization that the cosmic web is intrinsically dynamic" (87). Whereas we once thought of matter as particles and isolated entities, we now understand matter as comprised of wavelike patterns that move in constant interaction with everything in the matter's region of space. The essential quality of matter itself is an inseparable web of interconnections. There simply is no such thing as anything separate. Nothing, absolutely nothing, exists without being a part of a set or system of relationships. Any attempt to perceive things as separate and apart is an arbitrary and false separation.

Yet under most conditions our senses seem to tell us just the opposite. Thus we create a perception that there is "self" and "other." We learn about some "thing" and we view it as not really related to who we are. We create subject matter that seems to stand alone, by itself. In reality, however, there are no such divisions in life. Life does not create boundaries, we do. So we have the rather arbitrary divisions of botany and zoology, sociology and anthropology, geology and paleontology, when in fact the divisions are only defined, not real. Hence we create curriculum as if the world were made up of separate parts and we have come to believe the parts, and not the reality of the whole.

If we really think about what Capra's description of reality means, it calls into question almost all of our common-sense notions of what the world is like. Physicist Paul Davies (1988) says that "the new descriptions of reality that come from the new sciences "turn three hundred years of science on its head!" (22). Perceiving this reality is very different from our typical experience. The book, the table across the room, the tree outside, the bird on a limb that suddenly flies to another tree, and you, at the very foundation of existence, are not separate! Nothing has challenged our ability to understand our world more than this fact. How can we have unique and individual identities and yet be part of the same whole? The new sciences tell us that life as we know it is not only interconnected but inseparable. While it may be useful at times to view life within its boundaries and to employ mechanistic practices, the assumptions that need to be most prominent are those related to the essential wholeness of all things.

One of the ideas that helps us understand the concept of connectedness is the notion of relationship. A statement from the Four Worlds Development Project, an American Indian intertribal group, asserts that, "We can never know anything until we understand how it relates to everything else" (Bopp, et al. 1989, 26.) Compare this statement to the following assertion about quantum physics: "We cannot understand [subatomic particles'] properties without understanding their mutual interactions, and because of the basic interconnectedness of the subatomic world, we shall not understand any one particle before understanding all the others" (Capra 1991, 204). The world is essentially in relationship with itself. Just as your lungs cannot be understood apart from their relationship with the rest of you, other aspects of the world cannot be understood separate from the whole. And where do we draw the boundary of the whole?

As teachers, if we turn our attention away from independent facts to the relationships among those facts, we begin to allow our students to see a view of a more connected world, a world of relationship and meaning. If our curriculum and instruction continues to treat information about the world only in terms of its isolated characteristics, then we are teaching about a world that does not exist. The great quantum scientist Niels Bohr wrote, "Isolated material particles are abstractions, their properties being definable and observable only through their interaction with other systems" (Capra 1982, 137). The nature of our questions must change from "What is it?" to "What is its relationship and how does it interact?" The more we perceive and understand how everything is connected, the more deeply and richly we can experience the world. The world of connection is a world in relationship with itself.

One of the most significant aspects of connectedness we have learned from the new sciences is that we are part of the world we observe. In other words, there is no such thing as a separate observer. We are coparticipants in the ongoing creation of the world. Consider carefully the following explanation, again provided by Fritjoff Capra (1991):

> **Quantum theory thus reveals a basic oneness of the universe. It shows that we cannot decompose the world into independently existing smallest units. As we penetrate into matter, nature does not show us any isolated "basic building blocks," but rather appears as a complicated web of relations between the various parts of the whole. These relations always include the observer in an essential way. The human observer constitutes the final link in the chain of observational processes, and the properties of any atomic object can only be understood in terms of the object's interaction with the observer. This means that the classical ideal of an objective description of nature is no longer valid . . . In atomic physics, we can never speak about nature without, at the same time, speaking about ourselves. (68 and 69)**

Capra's quotation has two essential meanings for us: (1) we are literally inseparable from the rest of nature, and (2) everything we do and everything we are become creative aspects of the universe. In quantum science the identification of self-as-other is called *participant/observer.* In the very act of observing the world, we participate in its creation. Understanding that we are an integral part of the universe, we can view ourselves in a larger, more interdependent and participative context. This view is called *self-reference.* Whenever we alter the way we view the world, we do in fact change the world we are viewing. This seems almost counterintuitive, but it is part of the new landscape of reality that we are coming to know.

As we become increasingly aware of our connectedness to the rest of creation, every action holds within itself dynamic possibility. Understanding "self" within this framework means that we are part of every other self.

It means, too, that all selves are part of a single, indivisible whole—literally. The realization of our inherent connectedness with one another, with nature, with ideas, and with the spirit of all things manifests itself in our ordinary and daily activities, our professions, and the relationships in our lives. It is something we begin to know at a deep level, not just intellectually, but at the core of our being. Sam's poem expresses this sense of connectedness:

Your Story as Mine

Oh venerable tree
tell me your story—
in picture words that
linger,
in gentle movements
of an imperceptible breeze;
in the rhythms of your dance
of ordered chaos.

Let me savor the beauty of
form against sky;
glory in the shape of a configured past,
when seeds burst forth
from an underground night.

Let me know your story
as mine,
and mine as yours.
Heal the fracture of
my being
that perceives you as
removed from me—
as an object to behold,

as a chance encounter
waiting for significance.
Understand my pain of human arrogance.
(Do you see me crying
the tears of my race,
not appreciating your perfection
as mine,
and blinded by the ego of a constricted self?)

May our blood mingle
in a rite of passage
where harmony resides,
where my feet
are covered with earth—
seeking roots;
where my eyes are heavenbent
and our limbs
reach together toward
the dark expanse.

Help me know the memory
of my beginnings
when we were one,
and I was whole.

—Sam Crowell

Meaning vs. Sterility

Without a sense of connectedness, we tend to experience the world as sterile and empty. As educators, we are faced with creating and facilitating experiences that tap into the lives of our students, inviting them to participate in a world of exploration and self-discovery. Thomas Moore (1992) might call this "soulful" teaching. He wrote that "as long as we leave care of the soul out of our daily lives we will suffer the loneliness of living in a dead, cold, unrelated world. We can 'improve' ourselves to the maximum, and yet we will still feel the alienation inherent in a divided existence" (284). We think Moore speaks directly to our work as teachers and educators. Meaningful learning is connected learning. The more deeply we feel a connection to what we are learning, the more we are motivated to learn. Even more significant is that if self-reference (seeing the world as an aspect of our own participation in it) is a defining quality of a connected universe, then no matter what we learn, we are ultimately learning about ourselves. This truth suggests that the curriculum, no matter what subjects we teach, is sitting in front of us every day, in the living, breathing lives of our students.

Teaching for meaning relates to the Caines' (1997a) notion of felt meaning and deep meaning. Felt meaning is an "almost visceral sense of relationship, an unarticulated sense of connectedness that ultimately culminates in insight" (113). When we experience felt meaning there is a tie to what we have learned. Deep meaning refers to the fundamental purposes and values that organize our thinking. It includes intrinsic motivation, the ways in which we interpret experience, and our need to explore more deeply.

One of the teachers we work with was reading a story to her kindergarten through second-grade class about a flower garden. In the discussion afterward, she pointed out how the soil and water became part of the plants. Suddenly the class asked if the rain and the sun weren't also part of the plants. And if that were true, then what about the stars? The teacher became nervous about where the discussion was headed. She realized that her children had an intuitive understanding of connectedness, and the enormity of the concept came home to her in the middle of this lesson. She was overwhelmed and needed to divert the lesson to a safer place. The students, though, were thoroughly captivated by their discovery and the teacher planned to revisit the discussion in many other ways. She realized that she had been given a perfect opportunity to show that connectedness was an inherent reality of all life. She realized that by exploring the connectedness within a flower garden, we can explore our own connectedness. Donald Oliver (1989) shares a wonderful example of these kinds of possibilities. He describes a first-grade activity in which the students planted pumpkin seeds in milk cartons. They watched them develop and grow, noticing the various stages of change that took place. The teacher then created sentence strips for the children to arrange in sequence. For instance, one sentence read, "We planted the seed in soil." Another sentence stated, "The seed sprouted and developed leaves." The rest of the sentence strips related to the development of the plant and the eventual pumpkin. Certainly, we could say that this teacher encouraged observation, hands-on experience, relevant vocabulary, and skills of sequential organization. But is there a sense of connectedness that brings students into relationship with the pumpkin plants? For example, could a discussion include how the pumpkin seed might have felt as it stretched forth and first felt the warm sun? How does it feel to grow? Does the pumpkin plant like to be cared for just as we do? Would they think of the pumpkin plant differently if they gave it a name? The plant's purpose was to produce a pumpkin; what might be one of our purposes? Plants develop roots; what does it mean to be "rooted?" Oliver notes that plays and dramatizations that depict the life cycle of the pumpkin plant also could be performed. Of course, Oliver's observations open questions about life cycles in general. What is a cycle? Do humans participate in nature's cycles? How do cycles show endings and beginnings? What significance do cycles have for us?

If you think these questions are philosophical, some of them are. If you think they have no interest to first graders, think again. These kinds of questions relate what students are learning to their own lives. Questions need to be asked, they don't need to be answered. It reminds us of the kindergarten boy who asked, "Teacher, where does the sky end?" That question is about the wonder and mystery of life. We need to feel connected to what we are learning about. Otherwise learning begins to have less and less meaning. If we think about life only as an object, only in terms of getting through it, of survival, then what meaning does living really have? Surely we must reach for more than mere survival! The richness of life's meaning comes through our connectedness. The Orientation Three teacher feels these connections and makes them a part of the learning environment.

Embedding Connectedness in Our Teaching

The process of embedding is one of the most powerful tools teachers have, both to explore the scope of broader meanings and to examine more closely how a particular element relates to the larger whole. The word *embed* means to "make an integral part of." On the surface, this process sounds easy. Yet once again, the success is dependent on a perceived awareness of how one aspect of information or an idea is part of another.

There are two ways of embedding connectedness that we want to discuss. The first makes use of our senses; the second taps our ability to create symbols and metaphors. Both require us to see patterns, explore relationships, and construct meaning.

Understanding Connectedness through Our Senses

Let's take the familiar example of a leaf again. Imagine holding the leaf in your hand. You can see it, feel it, and use your senses to describe it. You may use these descriptions to understand the leaf as component parts or functions, that is, veins, cells, photosynthesis. We explore how these are "integral parts of" the leaf. We embed these elements into our understanding of what a leaf is and what it does. We may also want to see how the leaf is a particular component of the tree. In this kind of embeddedness, we move outward from the leaf to the tree. Again we may focus on purpose and function. Most often, we have a tendency to stop making connections at the point where we begin to lose focus on the leaf itself. But why? There is no reason for us to stop at any particular place. For example, we might continue to move outward from leaf to tree, to forest, to inhabitants of the forest, to kinds of forests, to bioregions, to atmosphere, to weather, and so on. Or, we might also look at insects that feed on the leaf, birds that feed on insects; the decomposition of the leaf, soil, bogs, marshes, and oil. Looking for ultimate connections, we may finally focus on the sun and the transformation of energy into living food that can be related to forests or the creation of oil and gas.

These connections do not in any way take away from a particularized understanding of the leaf. In fact, seeing the leaf in this broader context actually provides greater significance to its existence. Of course, so far we have only been trying to understand the leaf scientifically. What would it mean to investigate the leaf visually? Through prose or poetry? In terms of social and psychological implications? All these investigations may or may not be appropriate depending on the time, age, level, subject emphasis, and interest of students. Simply drawing attention to the connections, however, builds an ever-expanding context for students. Brain research suggests that the building of connections is essential to learning. When we divide information into ever smaller components, we often lose the context and thus lose the pattern of connections, making it more difficult for the student to learn. When both narrow and broad connections are embedded into whatever we teach, learning is enhanced. What is equally important in this particular example of the leaf is that a larger pattern has also emerged—the pattern of connectedness! The significance of this larger pattern leads us to a discussion of a second kind of embeddedness.

Understanding Connectedness through Symbols and Metaphors

Another way of perceiving the world is to understand it in terms of what it represents. This approach sounds complex, but actually we do it all the time. Whenever we describe something in terms of its general characteristics, we use abstract concepts. For example, the tree we see outside our window represents a category of things that have similar characteristics. When we refer to what we see as a "tree," we really mean that we are able to classify it among other such things. After a while we take for granted that there really is such a "thing" as a tree, when actually it is just an abstract idea to allow us to label and classify our world.

Consider the differences among a palm tree, a giant sequoia, and a bonsai. What we observe are incredible distinctions, yet we classify them each as "tree." These are concepts, categories that represent common characteristics. Again, although we often think of concepts as real, they are really just labels that represent a set of general characteristics that have become familiar to us. Hence, embedded in any concept are the characteristics we ascribe to it. And we can use those understood characteristics to give meaning to other situations that may not be literally true. For example, we refer to "the family tree" and the "tree of life." We speak of being "rooted in our beliefs." We describe people as "branching out" and we speak of "bearing fruit" in our lives. All of these are metaphors that express the idea of "treeness" in a unique way. If we play with this ability to give concepts meaning that extends beyond their usage, we begin to perceive the world consciously in both concrete and symbolic terms. If we embed meaning into what we experience, the richer our experience becomes. One caution: Metaphors are not truth, they are only new possibilities for meaning and insight. While metaphors help us go beyond the boundaries of concrete reality, they also need to be subjected to thoughtful evaluation.

It is important to understand that symbolic meaning is part of a creative process. The individual moves into relationship with an idea to discover if it has significance beyond its tangible reality. It is this process of moving into relationship and of going beyond that most applies to connectedness. Orientation Three teachers understand that exploring our connection to ideas at a deep level creates a qualitatively unique relationship to learning. These teachers encourage students individually or collectively to explore the possibilities of multiple meanings. They know that embedded in any idea are potential meanings that can be insightful, provocative, or even transformative. Of course, embedded meanings may be mundane or they may be quite profound. The more we can begin to perceive these potentialities for ourselves, the more we can help our students see them.

While all meanings are legitimate to explore, we are most interested in the kinds of meanings that lead to reenchantment, or a sense of connectedness. The reenchantment of learning requires an ability to perceive connectedness at many different levels and in varied contexts. Developing the ability to perceive connectedness and embed its meaning in the ordinary events around us is critical to becoming an Orientation Three teacher. If we as teachers begin to perceive how what we teach is related to the broader and more significant aspects of life, then we will be able to create a fundamentally different kind of learning environment. The following section is meant to examine the nature of connectedness more closely.

Principles of Connectedness

After spending more than a decade studying the implications of the new sciences, we realized that over and over again, in different ways, these sciences were telling us that deep connections exist everywhere in the universe. We began to identify principles that would make the nature of connectedness more apparent. We wanted to understand better the subtleties of connectedness so we could include them more deliberately in our lives and our teaching. We developed what we call "principles of connectedness" that focus attention on different aspects of the same thing—dynamic relatedness with the world. These principles emerge from a scientific context and have particularized meaning in that context. But they also can be used to begin to see connectedness in the ordinariness of life. We have used these principles in our teaching, in organizational development, and in our own journey toward reenchantment. We believe that one or more of these principles can be applied to any subject, at any age, and in any experience. They represent a fundamentally new understanding of life.

You may find that some of these principles seem to have an almost heartfelt tone. The truth is, the language of science and the language of the heart are converging in a more common understanding of the world. Such words as *purpose, unified field, consciousness, relationship,* and *wholeness* are all used in some form of scientific discourse today. This shift does not mean that science has taken on a new function; it still seeks to describe, understand, and explain physical reality. What is new is that it is increasingly difficult to separate physical and nonphysical reality. We find scientists in all fields venturing cautiously toward questions that were formerly the province of philosophy, psychology, and religion. Questions about the interrelationship of perception and knowledge, of knowing and being are becoming more common in intellectual discourse. We believe that understanding connectedness will provide a map to the new landscape that is emerging. We have seen the power of these principles in the lives of teachers, in the classrooms they create, and in the schools that seek to make them a conscious part of their organizational practice.

1. Everything is a part and a whole simultaneously.

We once gave a workshop where we wrote this principle on the board and boldly asked teachers to give examples. There was a long, heavy silence. Finally, a tentative example was offered. "A word is a whole and it is also part of a sentence." Then someone else said, "A sentence is a whole and also part of a paragraph." Suddenly examples flooded in. "A child is a whole and is also part of a family." "A class is a whole and yet it is also part of a school and a school is part of a district." "A finger is a whole and is part of the hand and so on." Most of the answers dealt with everyday kinds of experience. We asked if the principle could be applied to the subjects we teach and to classroom and school communities. For example, subject matter disciplines are actually wholes that relate the particular information that addresses certain questions or that is relevant to a common framework of ideas. Because of this exercise, teachers were able to see how the bit and pieces of information fit together to make sense.

Understanding particular information from the point of view of the entire discipline gives a new and different meaning to the information. Disciplines, though, also represent only partial understandings of larger questions and issues. For example, Sam once organized a special summer program for gifted high school students that looked at the topic of "technology" from the perspectives of many disciplines. Physics and biology were quite different in their approach and their questions. History considered the development of technology and its impact over time. An anthropologist explored early tools with the students and had them build campfires with stones and sticks. Sociologists considered the social issues that technology raised, and a psychologist dealt specifically with the stress of living in a technological society. A theologian raised questions of ethics that are particularly relevant in a modern world, and the students read utopias and distopias, and approached them as literature. In the end, the disciplines were seen as presenting only partial understandings of a much larger and complex issue.

The idea of simultaneity represents a partial understanding of a system. It is a way of seeing how things and events are related to other things and events. While we can create temporary boundaries, these boundaries are arbitrary depending on where we draw our imaginary lines. What once was defined with boundaries becomes part of a greater whole or a new configuration. This principle of connectedness becomes a pattern of perception that helps us understand complex relationships at any level. It helps us make sense of our world and our place in it. When we operate from this principle, we are perceiving the relationship of one "thing" to another; we are perceiving connectedness.

2. The whole is contained in every part.

To understand this principle, it might help to use the analogy of a hologram. A hologram presents a three dimensional image that seems almost real. Remember Princess Leah in *Star Wars*? Imagine if one could somehow freeze the image of the hologram onto a solid form and then shatter it into bits and pieces. If you were to pick up a single piece, the entire form of the image would be there. Scientists Karl Pribram and David

Bohm, as well as others, have used the analogy of the hologram to create theories in both brain research and physics.

The idea of the whole being contained in every part is found also in our understanding of DNA. It is part of genetic research and includes such imponderables as cloning. Remember the scene in *Jurassic Park* where DNA was taken from a mosquito found in ancient amber deposits? The entire form was re-created from a single DNA specimen.

Less remotely, however, let's look at some human examples that, although not purely scientific, illustrate something of the idea of this principle. Sam's parents even today use the southern admonitions "Remember who you are" and "Remember where you came from." They mean by these phrases that, wherever Sam goes, he cannot escape the fact that he is his family. The values he was taught to live by don't go away just because he lives in California or writes books or gives speeches. He is part of something larger than his own unique experience. We all have within us aspects of the whole culture, history, and social conditions of our time, which doesn't mean that these are experienced or expressed in the same ways. Nor does it mean that we don't reject or change according to our unique circumstances and personalities. It does suggest, however, that the whole of things influences the types of circumstances we address with our lives and in the critical decision points we may face.

"The whole is contained in every part" is a principle that asks us to perceive the embeddedness that is present in all aspects of life. It asks us to examine those wholes we create to see if they are merely our own assumptions or represent hidden dimensions that offer possibility and insight. An embedded world is a connected world.

3. The whole is greater than the sum of its parts.

We mentioned this principle to someone who asked "How could this be?" It would seem that simple arithmetic says that this can't be possible. How can one plus one ever equal more than two? It was R. Buckminster Fuller who demonstrated how this reality is practical. When he invented the geodesic dome, Fuller showed that the whole itself has to be counted. If you move any one part, the entire whole is affected. In a relational world, one plus one equals two plus the equation itself. In the human body, we are not just the cumulative addition of body parts, we are the interaction and functioning of those parts. This principle presupposes a relational perspective—a perspective of connectedness.

What this principle means for a teacher or for a school is that the focus of anything is on the interactive and relational qualities. Whether it is history, math, science, language, or social studies, opportunities exist to study the way ideas and concepts are related. This principle also can be applied to the students' interaction with the information. What is the nature of that interaction? If you group students, for example, in different configurations, the nature of the discussion changes. The points of view and understandings of individuals create a dynamism that makes each group unique, if not in the outcome, at least in the process of reaching the outcome. People's ideas, knowledge, and histories come together to create something unpredictable and dynamic. What happens is always more than just the sum of the parts. This principle helps us to see that connectedness is a dynamic quality and that the process of interaction itself is part of our new understanding of the world.

The establishment of community in a classroom or a school is a critical concern for Orientation Three teachers. What is the nature of the interactions? How genuine are people with one another? Is there a unity of purpose that people identify with and feel a part of? What is it that makes us more than just individual parts?

4. Inner and outer reflect each other.

There is a new understanding in the sciences that the essential qualities of any given material object are comprised of both the unseen inner dynamics of the subatomic world and the influences of the external environment. These inner and outer dimensions are engaged in ongoing interactions with each other, defining a world of constant, creative self-organization. Many have called this process coevolution because all physical reality is continually forming and re-forming itself.

David Bohm (1982) argues that our mechanistic view of the world places far too much attention on the external dimensions of life. He distinguishes between the inner and outer aspects of reality using the terms *implicate* and *explicate* orders: "The implicate order provides the commonality deep within matter, energy, life, consciousness. The explicate order of the so-called ordinary world of experience unfolds and displays the implicate" (in Wilber 1982, 196). In education we have been taught to place emphasis on that which can be observed, the external, explicate, or outer world. Our objectives must be in measurable or behavioral terms; our management strategies are directed to short-term behavior and feature most prominently external rewards and punishments; our standards and outcomes target objectified criteria as most significant. The three of us are not arguing that these things are always inappropriate, but where is the connectedness between these outer directed practices and the inner world of the learner, the participation of the classroom community and the relationship between these inner and outer dimensions? When we emphasize so completely the explicate order, we are in effect saying to students that it is the only order that exists. Once again, Bohm addresses this point eloquently: "In the old physics, matter (which was the only reality) was completely mechanical, leaving no room for mind. But if, according to the new physics, everything is enfolded in everything else, then there is no separation of domains. Mind grows out of matter, and matter contains the essence of mind" (194). The landscape of reenchantment requires us to acknowledge and build upon the inherent connectedness of the inner and outer, understanding that these are aspects of the same thing and cannot be separated. If we can offer our students creative processes that allow both dimensions to be expressed, we can begin to see the richness and power of wholeness. If we can build a climate of trust and community in which both inner and outer realities are recognized as authentic and meaningful, then perhaps our students will focus more on connectedness and relationship, rather than division and power over others.

If we can build a climate of trust and community in which both inner and outer realities are recognized as authentic and meaningful, then perhaps our students will focus more on connectedness and relationship, rather than division and power over others.

One of our graduate students shared with others in the class a way to introduce themselves to one another in a way that combined the inner and outer aspects of their lives. John had individuals bring some artifact of personal significance to share with the rest of the class. He placed a table in the center of the room, draped it with a beautiful cloth, and placed a few art objects on it. John explained that each person would be helping to create a "mesa" that would represent their unique stories and experiences, as well as their collective spirit. As individuals presented their artifacts and the stories behind them, you could feel the atmosphere change. What at first seemed like very ordinary objects became significant for everyone as the stories of happiness, love, tragedy, and hope were shared. Unexpectedly, some students broke into tears, others generated laughter, but all revealed inner qualities that touched the hearts of those who were there. The mesa became an example of the class's collective spirit, and even years later, students comment on the powerful effect that simple celebration had for them. A bond was established that was based on a deeper sense of who people were, where the inner and outer realities came together.

One of the most important understandings of this principle of reflection is the notion of self-reference. Everything we think we know is filtered through the lens of our experience. The inner reflects the outer. Therefore, the process of coming to know must involve distilling what it is that we have experienced. To test this, you can talk to your class for a few minutes about anything. Afterward, ask them to discuss what they felt, heard, imagined, or thought was interesting. Ask them what they thought was important to you, and ask them what was important to them. If your experience is like that of others, you will be surprised at the variety of impressions, interpretations, and images that were generated. The more complex our teaching and the more stimulating the experiences we introduce, the more variety you find. Orientation Three teachers learn to work with and use this expansion of meaning and make it a part of what is learned. In this way, no matter what our students are learning, they are also learning about themselves.

If we focus only on the external information, we will miss opportunities to address openly the skepticism, imagination, assumptions, attitudes, and questions that our students bring to the subject matter.

All subjects are reflected to some extent in the attitudes, likes and dislikes, and experiences within students' lives, as well as in how those subjects are taught. Years ago Sam's daughter, Chesley, sat doing homework when she burst out, "I hate social studies!" Sam was surprised and pointed out how much she seemed to love information about other cultures, history, and geography. Chesley responded adamantly, "That's not social studies. Social studies is doing the review questions at the end of the chapter!" We learn from this episode that children do not easily separate a subject from how that subject is taught. Even if students are interested and curious about particular subjects, it is important that they have opportunities to explore those interests and generate their own questions. In fact, it is participating in a subject that allows us to connect to it. If we focus only on the external information, we will miss opportunities to address openly the skepticism, imagination, assumptions, attitudes, and questions that our students bring to the subject matter. When the inner and outer are integrated, you will see a different landscape with new demands and new possibilities. It is a different way of seeing connections.

Connectedness as a Living Perspective

The very thought of connectedness has power. It is a concept that brings together things, events, people, ideas, and action. Being aware of the endless connections we are all a part of is a living process. More than an intellectual idea, it is a state of being, a way of ordering the priorities of our lives. Connectedness demands a living response, an active participation, and a sensitivity to an expanded definition of who we are. It leads us to look at the problems we face in a new way—in a way that honors the reciprocal and relational nature of the world. It calls us to become conscious of the meaning we create.

The mechanistic view of the world that has so defined modernist culture has created a mindset of fragmentation and isolation. Duane Elgin (1993) believes that "the reach of our technological power exceeds the grasp of our inner learning" (138). With our focus on the external world, we have forgotten that it is the human spirit that must also be nurtured. Technology cannot provide that nurture.

A culture built on a materialist foundation can say nothing to the human heart. We agree with Donald Oliver (1989), who notes

> **It is our thesis that humans are, in fact, part of all life, that life is part of nature, that nature is one domain within a broader universe, and that unless we feel—in a deep ontological way—these connections, we, as humans, tend to build destructive illusions of grandeur, to dream Faustian dreams of ultimately controlling all life, nature and universe. Our assumption is that without some intuitive sense of these connections, cultures and social systems lose their homeostatic balance between the separateness and the unity of being.**
>
> **The consequence of this loss of balance is a mixture of arrogance, as we seek to dominate a nature that stands outside ourselves, and the loss of our inner spiritual will, as we lose the feeling for what it all means. (58)**

Reenchantment is about renewing a sense of this connectedness and making it part of a new culture of meaning.

As educators we have an opportunity to bring this sense of connectedness to life within our curriculum and within our students. The challenge is to avoid what Alfred North Whitehead (1967) called "inert knowledge." Nothing is more boring than information that has no life, no context, no relationship to anything significant. In bringing a sense of connectedness to how and what we teach, we will enliven the world of learning and find a greater sense of joy and meaning in what we do. We will not only be preparing our students to "see with new eyes" and to be comfortable in an ever more dynamically complex world; we will also be planting the seeds for a new kind of culture, one that is aware of itself as a meaningful whole and that creates new patterns of unity.

A sense of connectedness is the spirit within Orientation Three thinking. While connectedness is a scientific reality permeating every field and discipline we know, it is also a way to experience the world. In experiencing connectedness, we begin to see it all around us in the events and observations of our lives. It is a life of participation, reflection, and creativity. As a living perspective, it is our guide in the landscape of reenchantment.

Process and Reflections

Personal

1. Continue the activity of making a list of your things to do, being aware of your feelings, questions, and issues, then responding spontaneously in the third person. Read to yourself your answers from the previous weeks.
2. Begin a journal that deals with connectedness. Spend a few moments each day focusing on your awareness of being connected to something in your world that has significance and meaning to you. First acknowledge the connectedness, then describe the feelings that accompany your awareness.
3. In a quiet place, gently relax your body, close your eyes, and focus intently on your breathing. Simply follow the breathing in and the breathing out for a few moments. Imagine the ocean tides following the same rhythm of your breath. Imagine the trees and animals taking in your breath and you taking in theirs. Imagine all the breaths of all the people sharing the same breath and breathing it out again. Imagine your connectedness with all that is. Then once again focus on your breathing in and your breathing out for as long as it feels comfortable. When you are finished, give yourself a few minutes, then focus on practical and concrete things to be done.
4. Apply one or more of the principles of connectedness to some aspect of your personal life. Reflect on that principle throughout the week as you encounter experiences in which it applies.

Group

1. In your ordered sharing, discuss what for you were the most profound issues expressed in this chapter.
2. Somewhere in this chapter we have written, "this isolation from our essential nature has resulted in a pathology we call 'the modern age.'" Do you agree? Spend some time to check out assumptions and reactions.
3. Mainstream American culture spends most of its emphasis on externalizing experience. How can we begin to honor the "inner landscape"? How is it possible to honor our physical reality, our intellect, and our larger inner reality?
4. Beginning with the group process, explore what the chapter discussion on embedding means to you.
5. Using the group process, share the meaning you have found in one of the principles of connectedness.
6. Apply one or more of the principles of connectedness to possibilities within your school organization.

Teaching

1. Choose some simple, concrete object that relates somehow to the grade level and subject matter you are teaching. (It doesn't have to be directly related.) In brainstorming fashion, explore with your students micro and macro connections. See if they begin to apply the same idea of relationships to some other specific aspect of what they are studying.
2. As a reflective exercise, use one or more of the principles of connectedness in thinking about what you are teaching. How does the principle connect to your curriculum?
3. Begin looking for connections everywhere and point them out to your students in a matter of fact way.
4. Apply notions of relationship and connectedness to your classroom community.

Soul Reflection

5

Reenchantment as *Wonder and Imagination*

> ***Until we accept the fact that life itself is founded in mystery, we shall learn nothing.***
>
> **—Henry Miller**

So far in this book, we have suggested that part of the journey to Orientation Three thinking involves being able to experience the joy of the ordinary and seeing the world as imbued with an aliveness that is part of us all. This sensitivity and awareness to the world around us, the students in our classrooms, and the possibilities that are yet to unfold are part of an essential quality that, with practice, can be developed and enhanced. An openness to joy invites us to participate in a connected world and feel a part of something greater than our own egos.

Exploring what connectedness means enables us to develop the perceptual "eyes" that make the fact of our interconnectedness visible everywhere in our world. The relationships in our schools and our classrooms take on more meaning. The curriculum takes on the possibility of depth and substance. We open ourselves to a more powerful and enriched way of experiencing life. For some, seeing the world in this way will seem intuitively right. Others will need time to reconcile this view of reality with previous outlooks and beliefs. The shift will be counter to the dominant modes of practice in our society and perhaps in your own lives. We use the term *perceptual orientations* precisely because the way we develop depends on how we "see" the world.

This chapter will explore how we might begin to create the conditions for a learning environment that supports Orientation Three thinking. Our first steps into a new perceptual worldview create a heightened awareness of things we thought were already familiar to us. Our former practices may take on more meaning or we may feel a sense of uncertainty and rejection about matters we took for granted. In either case, a dissonance is created that is both exhilarating and scary. The three of us have found that when we can experience our new perceptions with wonder and imagination, we can begin to participate actively in constructing a new reality and new possibilities. These attributes push us to respond more authentically to our own experiences.

If this is true for us as educators, it is also true for our students. Wonder and imagination present the potential for expanded meaning and creative participation in our learning. We will explore how these predispositions toward learning and experience can assist in our development as Orientation Three teachers. Part of our purpose is to be creatively active and responsive in the world around us.

Experiencing Our Humanity

Recently a group of us took a mountain hike during a full moon. The sun was setting as we began and the last views of red and purple faded in the evening sky. As dusk turned to darkness, the moon appeared over the rise of a mountain ridge. It shone so brightly we had to squint our eyes, and when it was in full view, we ran to the edge of some massive boulders. At first we were giddy with excitement, but there was suddenly a deep silence as we gazed at the beauty that enveloped us. Ridge upon ridge seemed to float on a gentle fog. The moonlight shimmered through trees and lit up the valley below. Craggy rocks displayed the character that time and the elements had created. All of us sat in silence, too full of emotion to say anything. Each of us was lost in our own world where the beauty of the moment merged with dreams and faraway thoughts. When we finally began talking, our sentences began with "What if . . . ?" "I wonder . . . ," "Do you think . . . ?" We were full of the mystery of the sky, the mixture of darkness and light that lay in front of us. We felt a close bond as if drawn together in space and time just for this single moment.

So often in trying to define and explain the world, we forget that a sense of wonder and awe is one of those human qualities that helps us experience what we are trying to explain. Our language too often becomes technical and specific, and we lose the power of the essence of it all. Ray Grigg (1990), a writer and former high school teacher, sees a close relationship between wonder, mystery, and understanding. He writes "Begin, therefore, with the mystery of the obvious, with the profoundly ordinary and the inexplicability of the simple. Understanding does not become wonder until the simplest and the lowest are amazing. Without wonder, understanding is not alive" (77).

The Relationship between Wonder and Meaning

As we have noted, Orientation Three teachers are committed to fostering the development of dynamical knowledge, felt meaning, and deep meaning. Meaningful learning penetrates to the life of the individual. In philosophical terms, it represents a transition from knowing to being. In other words, something inexplicable happens inside of us that affects our life. When learning becomes meaningful it is transformative.

So much of what we learn today is presented as an accumulation of facts. Even the word *fact* has a ring of certainty, finality, and objectivity about it. It is as if we were saying "end of discussion—this is the way it is." We three are not suggesting that you reject facts; however, we are imploring you not to end the discussion. Facts have little to say to us until we place them in a context of "What do these facts mean or suggest?" or "I wonder if . . . " or "Wow!"

We have all been frustrated during political debates when "facts" are thrown at us left and right, with the politicians often using the same information to draw very different conclusions. When we present facts as the end of knowledge, then we are implicitly suggesting that knowledge itself is sterile and unconnected to who and what we are. Then we wonder why so many of our students seem disinterested in learning. How can they not be, unless they have somehow bought into the game that the more they can accumulate, the more control and power they can wield? For information to become meaningful, we have to go beyond the facts to the source of meaning—ourselves. Human beings are creators of meaning.

The Wonder of Beauty

As we seek to develop a sense of wonder in ourselves and our students, let us first look at wonder as an awareness of beauty or as a kind of aesthetic perception. It seems that although much of what we consider to be beautiful may be culturally or personally derived, it is clear that humans find beauty deeply meaningful. If you have ever gone to a fireworks display, you may have found yourself giggling openly at the sight of multicolored lights creating beautiful patterns in the sky. Each new spectacle brings a collective "Ooh!" and "Ahh!" from the crowd. It is as if we were experiencing it for the first time. We put our children on our shoulders and watch the delight in their faces, knowing that innocent delight is one of the treasures of being human. Or you may have been moved to tears by a beautiful ballet, a piece of music, or an exquisite ice skating routine. The power of beauty is that it makes us feel wholly alive. It fills us with a kind of wonder that doesn't need words or concepts. We experience the moment full of amazement, and that is enough.

There is actually a kind of beauty within all the disciplines that we teach. In the sciences and mathematics, for example, there is a "wonder-full" quality of order and symmetry. Things seem to come together and fall into place just like a beautiful piece of music. Exploring questions that allow our students to discover this quality opens them to the process of trying to understand the mysteries of our world. Of course, equally full of wonder are the irregularities and complexities of nature. Thus we see the simultaneous reflections of simplicity and complexity everywhere we look.

Many famous scientists remark precisely about the beauty they find in their inquiry. Einstein comments on wonder, mystery, and awe, suggesting that it was not the facts that drove him, but rather the desire to be in the presence of the infinite through his work. Nobel Prize winner Ilya Prigogine compares working in science to being part of a living symphony. He writes of the experimental method as an art (Prigogine and Stengers 1984, 42). Constant choices are made concerning the questions that are asked. It is the pursuit of the question that allows the personal creativity and insight of the scientist to emerge.

The social sciences offer their own kinds of intrigue. As we investigate history, culture, social groupings, modes of governance, and the use of power, we are presented with a context for our thinking and actions. Why do we choose the economies we do? What effects do our decisions have on the intricate web of relationships throughout the world? How does the way I live reflect the unspoken assumptions that define me? There is beauty in these questions when they are removed from the abstract and placed within the context of our living. There is beauty in reading authentic letters of the past and feeling a sense of connection to real people who lived before us. There is a feeling of beauty when we can touch the artifacts of a culture or a distant time. To feel the worn smoothness of a tool or to admire the intricate designs of a Tohono basket—these experiences tap our imaginations and give us a gentle exclamation of beauty.

The humanities invite us to come to know the creative expressions of the past and to participate in the creative forms of our own time and place.

How sad when these subjects are driven only by analysis and critique that neglect the possibility to experience different forms and definitions of beauty. Can we recapture in a work of art or literature the questions that are relevant today for our own lives? Can we put our attempts to understand these questions beside others, marveling at the depth and substance of the human experience? The humanities invite us to consider who we are and to participate in a kind of mytho-poetic expression of our lived experience. In doing so, we strive to be connected not only to ourselves but also to our history, our art, our science, our religion, and our culture. Beauty and wonder become part of us.

Beauty makes us gasp, makes us cry, makes us feel both pain and happiness deeply inside. It sensitizes us to our experience in a way that conceptual analysis cannot do. As teachers, if we can perceive the wonder of beauty and create experiences where beauty becomes real in whatever we teach, then a state of felt meaning can be established. Merely asking if our students can see how beautiful or amazing something is begins to draw their attention to it. Exclaiming your own sense of wonder is equally alluring. Learning and understanding can be deeply enriched when they are accompanied by the wonder of beauty.

The Wonder of the Arts

When we think of beauty, we often think of the arts. An artistic approach to the world teaches us about the essence of wonder. There seems to be a growing awareness that there is much more to the arts than we have previously realized. The arts go beyond mere entertainment; they virtually allow us to experience the world differently. They create an alternative context in which new questions and perceptions emerge. In our work with teachers, we have found that the arts seem to pave the way for substantial insights and cognitive understandings. This finding is consistent with what we know about the brain and with specific research into the correlation between the arts and cognitive development.

The Center for Arts in the Basic Curriculum has compiled impressive evidence showing that skills developed through the arts can transfer to other subject areas. Indeed the arts can trigger multiple forms of learning. Studies have shown that both focused and peripheral attention on the arts improves performance in other subjects as well as on standardized achievement tests. For example, one study in 1993 reported that "students with experience in music performance scored an average of 22 points above the mean on the verbal portion of SATs, and an average of 18 points above the mean on the mathematical portion of the test" (3). Researchers at the University of California, Irvine, have established that having test takers merely listen to a Mozart sonata prior to an IQ test on spatial reasoning increased their scores by up to nine points over scores of control groups. The effect was temporary, but still real. Anne Gilbert (1997) conducted a study of 250 students from four elementary schools who used movement and dance activities to learn language arts concepts. These third-grade students increased their state tests scores by 13 percent from fall to spring. The district average actually showed a decrease of 2 percent! Perhaps most interesting in this study is that, the more teachers used movement and dance, the higher their students' scores. There was a direct correlation between the amount of movement and the percentage of increase on their language arts concepts test (11).

While test scores support the viability of the arts in terms of other cognitive domains, our interest in the arts is much broader. First, the arts epitomize many of the personal skills and attitudes that Orientation Three teachers seem to have. Second, artistic efforts are supported by an environment that includes the use of time, grouping, supportive camaraderie, active participation, critique and other feedback, the type of environment that helps teachers develop Orientation Three classrooms. Third, the arts respond to innate human needs for self-expression. They can be a bridge from our inner self to the world around us. Reenchantment comes to life through the arts. We experience the wonder of our own connection with the world.

The Arts as a Guide to Orientation Three Thinking

Orientation Three thinkers perceive themselves as active participants in life. They view themselves as part of a dynamic process that requires their full attention and awareness. Orientation Three teaching is rather like body surfing. You can't separate yourself from the wave and you make your decisions about what to do while you are in the midst of the experience. The arts, by their very nature, teach us to be open to these kinds of experiences. While one can develop technique and skill in an art form, one can never really control it. At some point there is a letting go. Interviews with various professional artists have taught us that a sense of surprise is one of the greatest joys of the artist. The interaction with the material or media; the playing out of an idea, a visual or musical image that one seeks to capture; the emotional complexity that is brought to life all eventually succumb to the process itself. The artist must ultimately be surprised. Not only does the artist seek to draw from the imagination, but the process involved in creating art is itself full of wonder.

These realizations are confirmed by teachers who have attended institutes by the California Arts Project. The California Arts Project designs arts experiences for teachers in music, dance, visual arts, and theater. The project's design team is comprised of a professional in the field, a university artist, a high school teacher, and an elementary school teacher. This team plans experiences in each arts discipline that engage the participants actively in the particular art. Many of the teachers who have participated in the projects designed by the California Arts Project have had little previous experience in the arts; others have allowed themselves to drift away from their involvement in an art form they once enjoyed. In either case, the impact of this experience has been significant. Some of the insights from participants show how their thinking is changed through this experience.

- *I've seen proof of how important expression through the arts is, of how such arts media are unique and critical to our well-being, of how the arts experience can bring people together in fellowship, of how crucial participation in the arts is—as opposed to consumption of them.*
- *It has re-confirmed the centrality of the arts to my sense of life's wonder and beauty.*
- *I've learned that I don't have all the answers; that I'm not expected to have all of them.*
- *I learned that all experience does not need to be planned fully.*
- *I observed the remarkable ability of all to adjust to on-the-spot, unforeseen situations. It was as if these situations were planned.*
- *The teacher became the student and vice-versa.*
- *As we became empowered, the participants began to take over the process, and the staff became the participants. It was as it should be.*

These comments indicate some important characteristics that Orientation Three teachers seem to develop as a natural part of their perception and practice. They include (1) the opportunity for deep participation in the learning process, no matter what the subject; (2) the ability to be fully present and flow with what is happening—planned or unplanned; and (3) the realization that ultimately the teacher becomes the student, and vice versa. Such characteristics begin with the way we perceive things and with the gentle acceptance of these ways of seeing and sensing the world.

The Arts as a Guide for Learning Environments

We want to discuss two ways in which the arts can play a role in our learning environments as we shift to Orientation Three thinking and teaching. The first role they play is one of a powerful part of the peripheral environment. The second relates to the attitudes and atmosphere required for high challenge, low threat activities.

If you were to walk into some of our Orientation Three teacher's classrooms (elementary or secondary) on a typical day, you would hear soft, relaxing music that accentuates a calm atmosphere in which students are busy working alone or in small groups on a variety of projects. You might smell a soft scent of vanilla from a fragrance pot on the counter. Looking around the room, apart from student work, you might see impressionist prints with their light hues of color and their dreamlike scenarios, or perhaps a variety of other artwork that is temporarily displayed. It is also quite likely that you would see green plants or a vase of fresh flowers that bring a sense of life and nature into the classroom. You would notice that the soft lighting of lamps is used to counterbalance the harsh glare of fluorescent overhangs. You may be there when the teacher brings the students together to emphasize an important point about the process or the work they have been doing. When the students return to their work, the music changes to a complex baroque pattern. You notice a difference in students' concentration, in their level of focused attention. Later, as a natural transition is about to be made, you observe that the teacher has selected a poem that is relevant to the larger ideas that the students are studying. There is quiet anticipation, and the poem is read dramatically to a piece of selected music. There is a silent pause and a brief moment of ordered sharing. All this is the orchestration of the learning environment to maximize the conditions that facilitate learning.

This description illustrates the conscious use of the arts to enhance the overall learning environment. From brain research we know that the peripheral setting can make an important contribution to learning. Orientation Three teachers from preschool to college make use of the arts for this purpose. The very creation of the atmosphere and the dynamic quality of selection and change are themselves a kind of participation in artistic creativity.

Another way to use the arts as a guide for bringing wonder and imagination into our classrooms and schools is to model the kind of atmosphere that supports creative participation. A friend of ours, Joseph Lyons, helps teachers and schools understand that creative learning environments require a safe, supportive atmosphere in which students can take risks. A former teacher at Juilliard, an orchestra conductor, and a theater director, Lyons uses the arts to build community. In such community, you simply lose all fear of doing it "wrong." There is no hint of ridicule and you are encouraged to let your creativity emerge. Lyons stresses that teachers must bring out the pleasure of creativity in the students, and it will spread into all of their other work.

To establish a learning environment that supports risks and creative exploration, we emphasize a related brain principle that stresses low threat and high challenge, which means that encouragement and the joy of discovery must fill the learning atmosphere. It means rethinking our notions of time, the limitations we put on difficult material, and our insistence on right answers. Instead, there is an emphasis on thinking critically, making good judgments, being aware of our own feelings and those of others, being able to work with a sense of purpose, and being able to adapt a variety of skills to address questions and problems. There is an attempt to create a learning environment that provides strategies for learning and for accomplishing self-determined goals. There is an ongoing expectation for active processing, on which our thinking, our approaches, as well as our products, come under constant reflection. Such expectation requires emotional safety and a high degree of trust and authenticity. If we perceive the need for this kind of emotional safety in a creative arts environment, then perhaps we can transfer those understandings to all areas of inquiry and exploration.

The Arts as a Human Response for Self-Expression

Humans have an inborn need for creative activity. Some researchers suggest that the need for artistic expression is as innate as the need for food, shelter, and sex. It may seem hard to believe in this need at first, but several fascinating studies lend much credibility to the idea. In Desmond Morris's classic study a group of chimpanzees were given paints, brushes, and canvas. The primates began creating works of art almost immediately. Although their paintings resembled a form of abstract expressionism, there was a rather high degree of originality to each piece. What was interesting was that the chimpanzees seemed to enjoy it so much they did not want to stop. They slept less, changed their eating patterns, and even seemed less interested in sexual activity in order to paint! It seemed undeniable that the need to express themselves in this way seemed as strong as any other physical need.

The researchers decided to try the same experiment with preschool children. Palates were set up and the children had complete freedom to create anything they wanted, with no direction or instruction. Very similar kinds of behavior were observed. The children preferred the expressive activity to other options and the range of originality was impressive. This experiment provided further evidence that the creative urge is almost innate. It seems to exist in all primates and suggests that it is biological in nature. Although this research has been around for quite a while, it is amazing to us that schools still exhibit the incredible lack of opportunity for creative expression.

There is a second part to this story that is equally fascinating and has special relevance to the dominant behavioral practices in schools. The researchers wanted to reinforce the creative behavior and began offering the chimpanzees rewards after they finished a painting. For a while it worked, then the interest in painting declined at an alarming rate. They no longer pursued the activity with the same passion, the amount of incomplete work rose, and some discontinued altogether. Then the researchers went back to the preschool teachers and asked them to tell each child "good" after each painting. In a short while, the children became much more tentative in their work. They began asking the teacher if they were doing it "right," started looking at one another's work more, and the paintings themselves lacked the previous originality and became more conformist! Hence, not only do these studies suggest that our need to create is perhaps an innate need, they also shed light on the dangers of our pervasive practice of behavioral reward systems in order to manipulate performance.

An inevitable question is "How does a teacher promote better work?" There is a story about a professional artist who worked with special education students. Their paintings were extraordinary and received great attention. When asked how he taught them, he replied: "I basically asked them three questions. What do you like about your painting? What would you change? What would you like my help with?" In other words, he chose to teach as they needed to learn and he used the context of their work to introduce new skills.

We three have found that instructional practices that incorporate the arts have almost universal appeal, even for students who don't necessarily see themselves as artistically talented. There is a dramatic increase in attention. There is a genuinely higher level of interest and engagement. Finally, the retention of information and the degree of understanding improve. There is a reluctance, however, for teachers to initiate some of these practices. When we overcome the fear and awkwardness, it won't take long to become convinced that the arts are for everyone.

For several years, Sam has asked teachers and teacher candidates in both elementary and secondary settings to engage in many different types of arts activities with their classes. Time after time these teachers and trainees come back surprised and astonished at what a difference it made in their teaching. They also are almost always astonished that they could do it. With a little practice, they get more and more skilled, and they find that they don't have to be professional artists to make art work in the classroom. What happens is that the students themselves become engaged. When wonder and imagination become a part of how we approach learning, then perceiving the world in Orientation Three terms is not far away. We want to introduce two art forms that have been especially successful and that have not been given much time so far: storytelling and dramatic creativity.

Storytelling

One of the most basic forms of communication is the oral tradition. The oral tradition was used to pass down history, science, religion, and a host of literary forms long before writing was possible or available. Perhaps as much as 80 percent of our communication is in the form of a story. Just consider coming home and telling about your day. It is full of "she said, then he said, then I said." We don't think about these as stories, yet they are narrative accounts of events that we sequence and present to others in our own personal ways, using our own language and expressions. The noted psychologist Jerome Bruner has suggested that, as infants, we develop a sense of narrative even before language is understood. Yet ironically, if we ask people if they consider themselves to be storytellers, most answer "no."

Try this experiment. Depending on the grade level you teach, choose a book or short story to read to your class that is relevant to what your students are studying. Instead of reading it, tell it as a story. If you can, vary your tone a bit, use some gestures, and speak with expression, perhaps imitating a character or some aspect of the story. Watch your students carefully for their reactions, their attention, their responses. If your experience is what so many others have been, you will be amazed at the difference in your students' focus. If you in turn have students tell the story to partners, you will find that their retention of detail is surprisingly high. Also you will find that they will begin to incorporate their own language and expressions, for as soon as they tell it, the story is no longer yours; it is theirs.

For variation, if you are teaching at all from a text, instead of having your students read the chapter, tell the content of the chapter as a story (it doesn't matter what the subject is, even math). Again, see if your students can replicate the high points in a story of their own. Then have them read the chapter if you want.

To personalize your relationship with your students, try sharing a personal story that is self-revealing in some way. Or to make a point, share an experience that made an important impact on you. When we humanize who we are, our relationship with students begins to change. The same is true for our students. When students are allowed to share their stories you will find a class that bonds with extraordinary closeness. Our pluralistic culture demands the sharing of stories. For example, we tend to take for granted admonitions and generalities that deal with prejudice and racism. Yet we don't disregard so easily someone's story. There is a concreteness about it that flies in the face of more general points of view. It brings us face to face with contradictions. It brings us into dialogue. If we are ever to understand one another, how we are different and how we are the same, we have to have dialogue. It doesn't necessarily solve problems, but it helps us look beyond them to the shared humanity of all of us.

There are endless variations and uses of storytelling, so do give it a try. Combine it with other art forms such as music, visuals, dance, and theater, and your classroom will be one that is "full of wonder"—and learning.

Dramatic Creativity

Actually, storytelling is a type of theater. If you are able to use stories, then it is a short hop to creating a dramatic form. Simply playing roles, taking one side or the other of a perspective, becoming a cell or molecule, being one part of an equation or another—these employ the imagination in learning. Again, Joseph Lyons (1997) encourages us to "trust the inner artist and bring the dramatic arts into your daily classroom practices no matter what grade level or subject you teach. It does not matter if you sing or act yourself, it only matters that you allow and encourage your students to do so. Create an environment for your students to express themselves through the dramatic arts, and learning will be accelerated, deepened, and retained more fully" (3). While increasing our own participation in these areas adds to the effectiveness of our teaching, the point Joseph is making is the importance of these activities for our students.

This kind of theater does not require a script or a stage; it is improvised, based on the knowledge of the subject matter. Learning can come to life when students act out historical events, selections from great literature, scientific processes, or mathematical formulas.

Harvard professor Donald Oliver (1989) relates the story of high school students who reenacted cell division through dance, story, and theater. Not only did the students understand the particulars of cell division to a very high degree, their expressive talents emerged, the community spirit increased, and their relationship with knowledge became more personal. Oliver stresses the importance of "reenactment" as a way to understand more deeply our connections to the natural world and to one another. Consider that all religious traditions throughout the world use reenactment as a way to convey the special meaning and significance of certain events in their traditions. Reenactment is a type of theater that takes the form of both replication and celebration. Something is dramatically replicated and its significance is celebrated. If learning can contribute to a celebration of the human spirit and our unity with Earth, one another, and the possibilities within us, then it can contribute to the reenchantment of ourselves and our culture.

Using the arts to respond to our need for creative expression builds a bridge from our inner self to the external world. In responding to that world, we are connected to it. We find part of our own humanity in the process. We become part of the wonder and awe that captures our imagination and brings creativity to life.

Twinkle On

Twinkle on, little stars in the nighttime sky,
Snowy mountains point fingers in your direction.
You are so close I can pluck you from the vast dark
If I stand on tip-toe and stretch high.

You have moved in your journey of the night.
The trees with silhouette shadows say their prayers
And I lie prone on the ground
Looking upward in wonder of your presence.

—Sam Crowell

Imagination and Creativity

A few years ago, Hewlett-Packard had a television advertisement that showed its consultants calling back to the office, saying, "I just had an idea. What if . . . ?" The company became known as the "What If" company. It portrayed itself as a company committed to creative problem solving, one that encouraged imagination throughout its organization. Coincidentally, it was consistently listed as a high-performance company with innovations in both management and its product line.

It is ironic that we hear and read so much about the need for individuals who are creative problem solvers and yet it is rare to be in organizations that actually encourage us to use our imaginations; the two go together. Imagination leads to possibility. We often kill imagination when we concentrate so single-mindedly on right answers or perfect products. There is no room for error, for trying something unique. Our schools rarely promote using our imaginations. In fact, more often than not, imagination is seen as annoying or distracting. Students are implicitly taught that it keeps them from focusing on the "right answers." This formula is a sure way to garner mediocre thinking and to kill that spark of wonder that compels learners and seekers to push forward.

We three believe that all intellectual activity requires a great deal of imagination. Whatever the subject matter or real life issue, intellectual activity is more than just a matter of gathering information and facts; it is creatively applying these elements in unique, often intuitive ways. We do not at all disparage the scholarship of seeking and gathering information.

In fact, we think that too little of that very activity actually occurs. Most often, information is either given or presented with little of the joy and fascination of discovery. On the other hand, we emphasize again that information should not be the end of knowledge. Focusing on imagination and creativity helps us to consider a greater range of options for students to use and apply information. If we can push beyond the limited expectations of most learning environments, we may help our students tap into the world of wonder, awe, and imagination.

Orientation Three teachers perceive creative opportunities in everything they teach. It isn't just that they approach their own work creatively, but that they also encourage and allow students to pursue ideas playfully, over an extended period of time. Creativity requires this sense of playfulness. The most serious of topics can be approached playfully if we remind ourselves that there is no ultimate right or wrong, only possibilities and process. In this way, the possibilities become alternatives, aspects of a puzzle where knowledge, reasoning, emotion, and intuition all come together. The "what if" question allows us to try more than one solution. There is a constant blending of imagination and creative possibility.

In addition to being playful, creativity generally requires time. To give students a thirty-minute project with the admonition to "be creative" is almost a contradiction of terms. To explain this concept more fully, in creative activity there is usually what is called an *incubation period* during which we ponder various approaches to our problem, or something that we want to explore with originality. That is why some of our best ideas might come to us in the shower or on a walk or in the garden. Creativity is made up of both conscious and unconscious processes. Students need incubation periods to be their most creative. Incubation is important, but for those of us who like quick and definite answers, it can also be scary and frustrating. Understanding this fear, we can help our students realize that uncertainty and "mulling something over" is often necessary. Another important point is that often our first attempts don't work like we thought they would. Here we have the opportunity to process what we like, what we don't like, and what we want to change. It may be that at this point additional information, research, or technical skills are required. If the project or issue is compelling enough, it may offer the most significant kind of learning, when what we know and what we imagine join together with our experience and purpose.

Finally, there is an important social aspect involved in creativity. Increasingly we find that the creative process benefits from an interactive environment. Rarely, if ever, do people work on complex projects alone. Almost always, there is a creative team in which each person brings her or his unique talents to bear on the conception and development of the work.

Whether it is an artistic, social, or scientific endeavor, teamwork is more and more a necessity in today's complex world. Stanford's Elizabeth Cohen (1994) uses this notion in a cooperative learning process called "complex instruction." Multiple ability tasks are emphasized as a way to affirm the contributions of each person in the group. In this way the status of each group member can be acknowledged and protected. Gardner's notion of multiple intelligences supports this kind of cooperative group task.

When creative work is being done individually, interactive support is especially important. What we mean is that students who are working alone must have an opportunity to share their work and explain what they are trying to do, how they are approaching the project, and why it is interesting or important to them. Others then are able to give supportive feedback, raise questions, and make suggestions. Each person receives the benefit of others' reactions, and everybody is exposed to a broader range of ideas and understandings. Social interaction, whether in a team context or as a means of support and critique, can be valuable to the creative process. As we know from the brain principles, the brain is social. Purposeful social interactions can optimize the conditions that support learning. This is also true in the creative process.

An attitude of playfulness, time to incubate ideas, and appropriate kinds of social interaction can all play important roles in supporting the development of imagination and creativity. Reenchantment connects us to that creative spirit within ourselves. We become aware of the wonder all about us and we are free to respond to that wonder with imagination and creativity. As we become Orientation Three teachers, we perceive humans as essentially creative beings. We help our students become aware of the wonder of the world contained in every subject. We find ways to unleash their imaginations and participate in the wonder of learning itself and the joy of living a creative life.

The Unfolding of Creative Order

Have you ever been a part of a group that was planning something? People start talking on top of each other. Idea after idea comes forth, sometimes being quickly rejected, other times being altered slightly. One person takes an idea and runs with it, and another person does the same. Someone says "What about this?" and continues to elaborate. After a while, the group is talking only about one or two of the ideas and has set the others aside. The particulars become more important now and one after another is added. Details are discussed as if some decision has already been made. The primary idea starts to take definite shape. Heads nod with satisfaction and someone in the group tries to summarize everything that has been "decided." A few clarifications are made. A point or two is changed. It is done.

What just happened? How did the chaos and messiness of the process described produce something that makes sense? It is part of the unfolding of creative order. Creativity is not linear. It is explosive. It seems to go everywhere at once, then it begins to settle into patterns that interweave around a sense of purpose. Something emerges that is anticipated but not expected.

When we sit down with a group to plan something, there is an implicit trust that eventually something will come about. We know before we start that it is going to be messy, but we understand that it will be all right. We trust that the process will lead to something that could not happen otherwise.

Orientation Three teachers have this same trust, that when the processes of creativity are opened up, something will happen that can be used for learning. What will unfold is a pattern of order that can be examined and explored. This trust is a necessary component of a creative classroom. There must be a willingness to let meaning emerge naturally and then to process the experience and the meaning in as many ways as seems appropriate. This willingness represents a major shift for most of us making a transition to Orientation Three thinking. Don't assume that we mean not being organized or well prepared, or that we are suggesting an "anything goes" kind of attitude. That would be anything but true. What creativity requires is a profound awareness of what is happening and the ability to tie in real experience to real curriculum in multiple ways. It requires being able to organize after the fact, not just before. We may start with a central idea or focus, but we let go of having to control it. With a clear sense of purpose, we weave everything that happens around and through the idea. It is easy then to elaborate, expand, or provide other information that is relevant. The learning opens up to a continued expansion, allowing more and more insights to be generated. A period of consolidation helps to solidify what is important and then opens it for further expansion. This kind of spiraling goes deeper and deeper into the experience as well as the subject matter. It makes possible the opportunity to explore that sense of connectedness and relationship that was discussed in chapter 4. It opens our consciousness to a greater form of creative intelligence.

We have found that central to this process of letting creative order unfold is a clear sense of purpose. Returning often and deliberately to the purpose keeps us focused on the meanings behind the experience. What we mean by *purpose* is not simply a specific kind of outcome, but the significant meanings that have engaged us in the activity in the first place. What is important about what we are doing? How does it inform us about who we are, how we are connected, and who we might become? What can we learn about ourselves, one another, the environment, and the decisions we will make about where to go in our lives? Purpose returns us to the questions of our humanity and our connectedness with the world. It opens us to the possibilities of reenchantment.

Imagining Possibility

Many have known for a long time that imagination can unlock the mind to consider new possibilities. People speak confidently of "following your dreams" and the power of will and determination as ways to activate something within us that moves us toward that which we desire. We know that the "placebo effect" is real; our bodies act as if the pills we have taken have active ingredients, even though they may in fact contain only sugar. We believe it to be real, so our bodies act accordingly. Perhaps you are familiar with research about the basketball team that had half their players practice free throws and the other half sit and imagine they were making the free throws, practicing only occasionally. The ones imagining making the free throws had a higher degree of success than the ones who practiced alone. Therapists have used visualization techniques successfully for years, and increasingly, such techniques are applied to improve personal performance and to complement the treatment of physical illness. The effective use of affirmations to achieve personal change is documented in several statistical studies. (See Leonard and Murphy 1995.) When we open our minds to imagining possibilities, we open it to change. If we focus only on the limitations confronting us, we will be forever held back by our own boundaries of belief.

Possibilities can emerge from a sense of wonder and creative participation. As part 2 ends, we hope that you will realize the power of the imagination. We have presented some of the dispositions and "ways of seeing" that are part of Orientation Three thinkers' approach. The paradigm that determines the way we view the world is changing. It is already affecting all our institutions and what we know about the nature of reality. Our challenge is to navigate this new perceptual landscape, to encounter its possibilities, and to create a new world. We need to support one another on this journey, and above all, to share what we learn. Each of us can begin by imagining for ourselves the immense possibilities of a world that rediscovers its connectedness, that finds joy in the ordinary wonders of human experience, and that learns to participate creatively in the world of tomorrow. We can come to understand reenchantment at an intuitive level, where knowing becomes being.

Perhaps even more significant, we can help our students connect to the possibilities of their own lives. It is the fatalism, or the belief that things cannot be different, that most endangers the sense of possibility. For many, there is an absence of positive goals, and they do not see that their lives can be special gifts to the world. Indeed, how many of us, as we look out over the students who walk into our classrooms, really believe in our hearts that their lives are filled with possibility? Yet years of research show that this kind of belief and expectation is absolutely essential to our students' accomplishment. A psychologist friend and brain researcher recently shared with us that some studies have indicated that one of the highest predictors of future success is the hopes and dreams of a mother for her yet-to-be born child! It makes us wonder about the power that each of us as teachers has to lead students to the threshold of their own possibility. Can we share our dreams and hopes for them as persons and the possibilities that can be manifested through their lives? Can we help them imagine a world as it might be?

A New Beginning

Can I return to the mystery
of the mountains—
whose peaks look far into the horizon
and see new possibilities
as floating cloud dreams forever changing—
in the shifting breeze?

Can I recapture the mystery of ocean depths,
where life overflows with dream creatures
of beauty and terror,
whose cycle of the tides
mirrors my own breath?

If I walk toward the open light,
will I come to the field of a new beginning
and know myself again as part of you?
And if I make an offering to you
will you take me again to the center of my humanity
where the goddess tells her story
and heaven descends to receive it?

Let us write a new story
of our journey to wholeness,
a new story expressed in our art,
shared in our songs,
and lived in our lives;
a new story of a new beginning.

—Sam Crowell

Process and Reflections

Personal

1. Continue your list of daily tasks, issues, and responses. To what extent are you aware that the answers you seek are often part of your intuitive inner knowing?
2. Continue your journal of connectedness. Pay attention to the development of your perception and insights. Are you beginning to see the world in a different way?
3. Engage in some artistic activity of your own. It does not have to be elaborate or a highly developed skill. Sing to yourself; write a poem; beat out a rhythm to music on the radio; dance to a favorite tune; do a sketch or drawing; select a poem and read it out loud with dramatic flair. Whatever you choose, do it several times this week until the awkwardness and self-consciousness begin to fade. Don't be critical; lose yourself in the activity and have fun with it. Whatever you do, don't try to do it "right"; just enjoy it.
4. Continue to do the imagination exercise described in chapter 4's activities.

Group

1. Beginning with the group process, "unpack" the metaphor "teacher as artist" to explore possible applications for practice.
2. Try other metaphors such as "teacher as jazz musician," "teaching as improvisational theater," "teaching as modern dance." Discuss the kinds of skills and abilities teachers might need if they used these metaphors as models of teaching. How would using these models change what happens in schools?

3. What are your hopes and dreams for your students and the world you hope they create? What do you do to bring these to their consciousness?
4. As educators, we often tend to think and focus either on the arts, creativity, and feelings, or on rigor and high intellectual content. How and when do we combine the two?
5. We say that experiencing dissonance is critical to new learning. In what ways do you agree? Disagree?
6. What does "experiencing our humanity" look like in your professional world?
7. What does it mean to move from knowing to being? Check out your assumptions.
8. Throughout this book, we have referred to Orientation Three thinkers and teachers. Is this concept clear to you?
9. Do you have time to express an "attitude of playfulness, time to incubate and appropriate kinds of social interactions to support the development of your imagination and creativity"? What would it take to create this time for you? For your students?
10. What do we mean by "the unfolding of creative order"?
11. What problems are you currently replacing with possibilities?

Teaching

1. Try some of the suggestions made in the storytelling and creative dramatics section of this chapter. Make sure you do them several times to begin getting a feel for what they require. If you already do these kind of things regularly, try some variations. Use masks. Create alter egos. Use special lighting, different music, visual elements, or artifacts.
2. Use a variety of nonpopular music during transition times in your classroom this week. During work times, play some baroque or Renaissance selections.
3. Include some "what if" questions in your teaching this week, and create some possible scenarios for students to consider.
4. Choose something from your classroom community that merits celebration. Create a low-scale celebration that emphasizes something meaningful to the community. Let the students lead in the planning, given your parameters.

Part 3

Approaching Our Work

Part 3 shows how our new perceptions can be applied to how we work and to new ways to understand learning environments. If we are serious about creating classrooms and schools in which students are engaged in dynamical learning, then we may have to consider other ways to approach what we do. The purpose of this section is to highlight some of the abilities and skills that can assist us in being effective in these new kinds of environments.

Probably no issue is more central to the way we organize what happens in schools than control. When we understand learning environments as complex adaptive systems, however, the issue of control gives way to other considerations. We move, instead, to questions of relationship and community. The way learning takes place and the way we make decisions change as we understand the implications of working within systems that are dynamical and self-organizing.

The deepening of our own knowledge of content is increasingly necessary as we move away from textbook approaches to learning. Seeing the big picture requires a different approach to content that emphasizes concepts, ideas, and meanings. Expanding cognitive horizons means being able to guide our students to see the relationships in what they are learning to other areas of the curriculum. It also means delving into the significant questions of life that bring us face to face with our own humanity. Finally, the big picture is about where our understandings of the world might lead and why learning itself is so important to the futures we create.

All learning is personal. Thinking about our own learning empowers us to participate in the creation of self. The question shifts from "What do we know?" to "What kind of persons (teachers) will we become?" When we consider issues of self-reference and process, we perceive ourselves as active agents in the world. Approaching our work with these perceptions in mind helps to create a learning environment that is personal and dynamic.

Letting Go

6

Reenchantment as *Learning to Let Go*

From Control to Relationship

> ***Our attitudes are not yet tuned to valuing participation and social integration, or to accepting states of flux and becoming. The issue of interconnectedness has not yet penetrated our emotional responses, and certainly not our values.***
>
> —Suzi Gablik

The significance of reenchantment is "remembering" the roots of our humanity, the simplicity of joy as we become more aware of the invisibles beneath the surface of ordinary events, sensing and affirming our connectedness to Earth and to one another—to all things—and participating in the wonder of life as creative beings who imagine possibilities. Perceiving the world in these ways, we begin to live our lives differently. We also begin to notice the contradictions of institutional practices that are based on different perceptions and assumptions about the world. We become aware of our own internalized contradictions, as well. Seeing with new eyes makes it possible to recognize the landmarks of a developing cultural paradigm. A paradigm is the way in which we view the world. When we change our perceptions of the world, our approaches to living in the world also change. Therefore, whether a particular instructional method "works" or not is often dependent on the nature of our perceptions. What would be counterproductive in one situation suddenly becomes effective because the way we think about the context has changed. When we shift the way we see the world, new approaches seem not only natural, but almost obvious.

This chapter addresses one of the thorniest issues for teachers who are journeying to Orientation Three thinking—the issue of control. It is so pervasive in our thinking and practice that it affects almost everything we do. It raises questions about the very nature of what we mean by the word *teacher.* We are not going to argue against control per se. That would be ridiculous given the pervasive assumptions that characterize our schools and communities. Our point will be that once you change your assumptions, control is really not a very important issue any more; the more important focus is relationship. Within the context of complex adaptive systems it is not possible to control anything. Therefore we need new kinds of skills to understand what is happening and to be able to navigate in these kinds of systems. First, the three of us will examine why changing our assumptions is so imperative; then we will consider important understandings that help us approach our work in a different way.

Assumptions and Beliefs

Have you ever watched toddlers play "school"? How do they know even before they enter school how to play teacher and student? We have watched them tell the "students" to behave and sit down and do what "the teacher" tells them to do in order to "learn." We have also watched the "students" be either rebellious or obedient depending on how they want to play out the scenario. It's cute to watch the exaggerated antics, but if we look at most classrooms today, you will inevitably find grown-ups playing out this scenario in earnest. The teacher is in charge. The teacher decides what will be learned and how it will be presented. The teacher is the one who gives the information that everyone should know, is the one who seems to have all the answers, and is the only one who evaluates student work. It is the students' role to be obedient or otherwise face the consequences. They are to absorb the knowledge and show that they have "learned." They are to buy into the rules of the school that are there for their own good, and despite their backgrounds, culture, language, or experiences, they are to understand that school knowledge and the culture it represents is the only knowledge that is important.

For many, to think that teaching can be anything other than as it is in this scenario is absurd. Importantly, it is when we think that something cannot be otherwise that we should realize there are unexamined assumptions driving what we do. When we think in that way, we function on automatic, and all our questions and concerns are about doing what we "think" we ought to do better. The standards of practicality are used to determine which techniques help and which do not. But we never question the premise of the assumption. We cannot even consider that it could be otherwise. No matter what new innovations may be available, if the assumptions behind our practice are not challenged, nothing will really change. Even if we use new approaches, they are made to conform with our habitual beliefs about how things must be.

Living on the edge of possibility means that we have an organized and authentic philosophy of learning and teaching that allows us to use, invent, and create approaches that apply what we know about learning.

One of Sam's students recently commented that she had wanted to be a teacher for as long as she could remember. She would play school with her friends in much the same way as we described above. She was always the teacher. The student was beginning to realize, though, that her little-girl ideas about teaching were changing the more she confronted her assumptions about teaching and learning, which is exactly what is necessary if we are to journey into Orientation Three territory. We have to first confront our own deeply held beliefs and the beliefs that are entrenched in what we call *schools.*

Living on the edge of possibility does not mean that we keep inventing new strategies. It means that we have an organized and authentic philosophy of learning and teaching that allows us to use, invent, and create approaches that apply what we know about learning. At its heart, the reenchantment of learning is far more than one more approach to teaching; it is a new way of "being" a teacher.

Perceptual Differences

If we want to consider creating new kinds of schools that focus on learning, on connectedness, and on the creative potential within us, we will need to understand the power of our perceptions and the effect they have on school communities in the midst of change. All of us have had experiences in which someone else participated in the same event we did, but interpreted their experiences entirely differently from the way we interpreted ours. Former president Jimmy Carter and his wife Rosalyn found out just how real this phenomenon is when they tried to write about their common experiences in the White House. They ended up disagreeing so totally about what actually happened, they wrote at opposite ends of the house and would only communicate via computer about their writing. Ultimately they published the book with separate chapters entitled "Rosalyn Carter's Story" and "Jimmy Carter's Story." They both agree that this experience was the closest they ever came to understanding why people divorce.

When we speak of change, we mean both expanding who we are and taking on board new mental models of what is most significant.

Differing views of the same thing can provide opportunities for understanding and learning, but they can also enmesh us in heated discussions and angry confrontations. Differing views can provide a vehicle for greater understanding, but there must be a forum in which perspectives and fears can be shared and where there is a commitment to explore other possibilities and learn from one another in the process. The necessity of such a forum is one reason we approach school change as a group process and why we encourage schools to create a learning community in which our perceptions can be explored in a supportive atmosphere.

Perceptual change is about expanding and articulating our deeply held beliefs about teaching and learning. Obviously this articulation requires much more than simply acquiring a new strategy. It is about seeing how new strategies and teaching approaches naturally emerge out of a shift in our assumptions. When we speak of change, we mean both expanding who we are and taking on board new mental models of what is most significant.

Why Is Shifting Our Perceptions So Difficult?

Perceiving the world differently is exciting, but it is also difficult. There is an opening up to the possibilities of growth and expansion, but with that opening comes uncertainty and awkwardness. Just like a new plant bursting its way into sunlight, its roots are still shallow and its stalk is spindly. There are also other factors that make personal and professional growth difficult.

Beliefs are tied to identity.

We are our beliefs. They form a critical part of our identity. In the musical *Man of La Mancha*, Don Quixote repeatedly addresses the prostitute Aldonza as his "beautiful, ideal Dulcinea." Aldonza tries to convince him just how useless and hopeless she is and moves through extreme anger and frustration as she tries to get him to corroborate her own vision of herself. Eventually she does begin to take on his vision, but only at a terrible cost to Don Quixote, who bears the brunt of her fear and anger at letting go of a deeply ingrained view of who she is.

A more positive example is provided by the beautiful and perennial book *Hope for the Flowers* (1972) by Trina Paulus. In this work, Yellow leads Stripe into his necessary but scary metamorphosis from caterpillar to butterfly. Real change, therefore, means more than changing beliefs; it means moving beyond the old me and becoming "bigger" and "more." One of our teachers put it this way: "I always believed that this is the way you teach, but I began to believe everyone else. This process of change is like shaking off all the 'doo doo' that covered up my own inner beliefs."

The nature of our beliefs is personal.

Although we all share beliefs with some people, what we deeply believe about something is inevitably sacred and personal. Try asking fellow educators why they do things in a particular way. Why, for example, do we organize teaching on the basis of time as organized by the school bell? Why don't we organize learning on the basis of student understanding and meaning, instead? The mere idea that such a thing should or could be done will inevitably be met with resistance because our question challenges deeply held beliefs and practices that educators may hold dear. Because our identities are so often wrapped up in taken-for-granted beliefs, we may interpret such questions as a personal challenge or criticism.

Espoused Beliefs

Espoused beliefs are statements and actions that reflect what we would like to be true or think others expect to hear or see. They are often reflected in oral and written agreements that may or may not be consistent with what we deeply believe or actually enact in our moment-to-moment responses. Espoused beliefs are in mission statements and official documents meant to describe or establish common actions. We have all participated in one form or another in creating these beliefs, only to find that when we look closely at how they are implemented, the statements and our actions rarely, if ever, mesh.

What we say is often what we want others to hear. What we do can we can also base on the beliefs of others or "experts." Inevitably it takes identifying our actual beliefs before we can make new learning dynamic and meaningful for us and our students. For most people, mental models remain unconscious. As a result, these people subsume new approaches to the old beliefs. In these cases, individuals often claim that they have changed, when a closer look shows that there is a gap between what they espouse to believe and what they actually do in moments that are "off stage."

When we act consciously and congruently with what we believe or feel to be true, then we become authentic. Becoming authentic ends up being a lifetime work for most of us, but *authenticity* tends to describe Orientation Three teachers. They trust in their own abilities to face the unknown and use it as a springboard for challenging themselves and their students into learning. They encounter their practice as a way to bring to life their assumptions while having the ability to allow someone else to follow his or her own truth. They continually examine not just their practice, but what their practice tells them about what they really believe or are holding onto despite beliefs to the contrary.

Trust and authenticity relate directly to how we develop relationships in the school and classroom. Paradoxically, we affirm ourselves and "give up" ourselves at the same time. The remainder of this chapter will deal with understanding the process of this letting go. One of the actions that helps us become comfortable with such a step is seeing ourselves as part of a complex adaptive system. When we understand how a system works, we can begin to consciously apply this system in our classrooms and schools.

Creating Brain-Based Learning Environments

As we have refined our understanding of how the brain-based principles can be applied in everyday situations, we have become more and more aware of the disparity between learning environments that encourage substantive, deep, meaningful learning and those which, in many cases, actually impede learning. What we have observed is not necessarily surprising, but nonetheless, it confirms the use of brain principles as guides to both expanded learning capacity as well as improved learning performance. When teachers used the brain principles to guide their decisions, they found that the nature of the learning environment changed, not because someone told them to change it, but because the learning needs of their students demanded it. As the changes took place, the kinds of skills and understandings needed to make them work became different from those in which the teachers had been trained. Some teachers intuitively mastered these new requirements. Some used their training in various innovations to make their own connections. Others struggled, caught in the middle between what they had been taught and what they now wanted to do. What was needed was a way for them to understand what was taking place so they could make intelligent decisions to complement their intuitive skills.

While this need was certainly true at the classroom level, it was perhaps even more apparent at the school level. Bright, dedicated administrators wanted to support their school's progress toward brain-based instruction, but found that their understanding of school organizations did little to help them. When we began sharing our understandings of complex adaptive systems with the teachers and administrators who were trying to create these dynamic and challenging learning environments, there was an immediate recognition of the application of these understandings. Together we have tried to build upon the insights that are most relevant to the learning environments that are guided by what we know about learning and the brain.

Dynamical Self-Organizing Systems

Our schools and classrooms are complex adaptive systems. They function in dynamical, self-organizing ways. When we shift our assumptions to create more authentic learning environments, we deliberately place the system in an adaptive state of disequilibrium, which is a necessary condition for change and deep understanding to occur. One of the essential things for us to recognize about these kinds of systems, and especially those in which disequilibrium is present, is that they self-organize. In other words, disparate patterns and information appear to flow in random disarray until, mysteriously, order begins to emerge. This order is not just a leveling out, but is rather a distinctive emergence of a new state of being. Learning to work with self-organization changes the way we perceive what we do. We see ourselves as part of the changing environment and yet we are able to remain grounded in a sense of purpose and identity. This duality is not always nice and easy, but it places us in a position to respond and let go at the same time.

Self-organizing, dynamical systems are everywhere in our world. A river is one example. The life of a river seems so steady and constant as we gaze from its banks on a hot summer's day. The gentle splash of water that laps the shore seems timeless. What appears so steady and unchangeable to us, however, is actually much more dynamic. The river's life is filled with turbulence and uncertainty, with change and sameness. The river is constantly rearranging its environment and adapting to that environment, as well. It is gathering silt or clearing and deepening its bed. It adapts to the changing amounts of rain, of melting snows from the hills and mountains. It adjusts to the droughts and evaporation from the sun. In some places, water skims over rocks; in other places, it is contained by them. Sometimes the river surges into foamy white water with incredible force and speed. It almost seems to play when it jumps from rock to rock, then in another place we see it almost sleeping in idle pools where everything is at peace. It shows us all these faces as it continually responds to its environment. In spite of this constant presence of change and adaptation, unless it dries up completely and forever, it remains a river. There is a constancy of purpose and function; no matter how much it changes, it goes on being a river. If you are the river, you must become different as each new situation demands. The river we have described is a dynamical, self-organizing system.

Self-organizing systems must maintain both change and stability, which requires an influx of novelty, balanced by periods of consolidation. Most biological organisms require a great degree of innovation and creativity. Without these elements, they die. Briggs and Peat (1984) note that in living systems an "openness to fluctuation also means a greater, closer, more intimate connection with the flux and flow of the environment. Increased autonomy is paradoxically related to an increased . . . openness, which widens and loosens pathways between what is 'inside' and 'outside' the structure" (182).

What the statement suggests for us is that optimal learning conditions require creativity and open-ended experiences in which new information and skills challenge the learner's previous understandings and mindsets. Integrated constantly into this process is the need for deep consolidation, application, and further exploration. In brain-based terminology, this consolidation is called "active processing." We understand the nature of our thinking as well as the information. As a result, we may see ourselves as more autonomous; this autonomy is almost exactly what has happened to our Orientation Three teachers as they learned to trust the process more implicitly and grew more authentic in their relationships with others. It is also what has happened with their students. As we understand better the nature of dynamical, self-organizing systems, we become more comfortable with open-ended processes. We can pay attention more closely, be aware of the questions and issues that are most relevant to address, and plan ways to consolidate new learnings that build upon their experiences and insights. What happens is that we begin to use self-organization as a way to deepen and accelerate learning.

Some Scenarios

Imagine a learning environment in which all the desks are in rows facing the front of the classroom and the teacher is presenting some information. This situation is relatively controlled, although even here, the teacher is having to constantly monitor the attention of the students to make sure they at least "appear" to be listening and absorbing. The teacher may also be responding to questions, initiating discussion, or checking for understanding. So the teacher is having to respond to each of these situations as she perceives it. In spite of these constant adaptations to the environment, there is little opportunity here for the type of self-organization that we have described to occur. The students are relatively passive externally, although it is very difficult to know their inner state. Here, understanding self-organization does not help in any substantial way. (By the way, there are certainly many times when this type of setting is useful and effective, although for long periods of time or as the only mode of instruction, it is quite limiting.)

Let's alter the situation to one in which the teacher rearranges the desks in groups of four. She assigns the same task to each group, and the task will result in similar products that she will then grade. The task involves a limited number of skills and the students should have all the information they need available to complete the task. In this situation, there is still a great deal of control. The teacher has set tight boundaries about what is or is not acceptable and the task is not particularly open ended. Typically in this situation, there are also time limitations and restricted behavioral conditions. Nevertheless the approach that each group takes to complete the assignment will differ. The teacher no longer can monitor the group behavior in the same way. She must also rely on the groups to monitor their own performance to some degree. There will also need to be some consolidation and feedback to tie the assignment into the larger instructional purpose. Self-organization is increased from the previous situation, but remains at a low level because the overall assumptions about teaching and learning have not changed.

Now let's suppose the teacher decides to create heterogeneous groups of four or five students. She gives the students an open-ended problem to solve that will encourage them to use many different types of skills and abilities. The problem also requires that the students pool their talents and perspectives in order to decide how to approach the problem. They may need additional information; they may need to learn a particular kind of skill; they may need some parameters to guide the scope of their task. There is now a mixture of open-ended possibilities, many different kinds of information that may be requested, and a variety of self-contained interactive groups that are likely to be doing very different kinds of activities. In addition, the teacher may want to periodically interject new information, questions, clarification, and reminders. To an onlooker, this situation may still appear to be orderly and well managed, yet the level of self-organization has greatly increased from the first two scenarios. It is impossible for the teacher to control the learning situations in the traditional sense. She now must operate within the learning environment, in tune with it, with a different kind of awareness, with different intentions, and with different questions in mind than were necessary in the previous scenarios. The issue of consolidation is a large one and the range of possible learnings is exponentially greater in this scenario than in the other two. The teacher clearly is operating with a different set of assumptions and her challenge is to allow and encourage the open-ended exploration while maintaining a clear focus on and purpose for the learning task. She finds that the more she lets go of the need to control what happens, the more she needs to be keenly aware of a wide variety of relationships and be able to build upon them when appropriate. She finds herself waiting for just the right time to intervene or make a point or to interrupt the process for a brief presentation. She requires a whole range of new understandings and skills to be effective in this kind of learning environment. Both she and the students are now in different kinds of relationships and all are part of the larger experience. This scenario depicts a high level of self-organization. The potential for learning in this environment is very high, given what we know. The challenge for both the students and the teacher is also high.

Characteristics of Self-Organizing Learning Environments

In *Learning as a Way of Being,* Peter Vaill (1996) has called environments that are high in complexity and self-organization "permanent white water" situations. As a specialist in organizational development, he suggests that permanent white water situations are the norm and not the exception. He asserts that smooth-running, highly controlled business environments are "intrinsically invalid." They do not reflect what is needed to operate effectively in an interactive and interconnected world.

The three of us, of course, are saying the same thing about education. Schools and classrooms that are organized with mechanistic assumptions and feature most predominantly the delivery model of instruction are essentially not valid as environments that are high in learning potential. If we want to apply what we know about learning and to expand our possibilities as humans, then we will need to create dynamical, self-organizing learning environments. Teachers and administrators who co-create and live in these environments will need to be aware of the different kind of landscape they inhabit. We want to discuss three elements that Vaill describes as characteristics of "permanent white water."

Permanent white water conditions are full of surprises.

When the conditions for self-organization are high, there is no way to predict with any certainty what will happen. With experience you begin to be aware of patterns that seem to consistently occur. Just when you think you have it, however, something will happen out of the blue. Being open to and expecting surprise lets you enjoy the challenge of each new event. An engaging and significant central focus will help you pull together most surprise events into something that extends the learning. The principles of connectedness discussed in chapter 4 are particularly useful in these occasions.

They provide a larger dimension of understanding that relates to anything that happens. There is an inherent sense of orderliness that becomes apparent. Trust that there is no such thing as an unrelated event, and you will be able to see the connections and make use of them. Being well prepared means something very different from the traditional kinds of planning we have been taught. It means delving deeply into the substantive nature of the content, the significant patterns that are evident, and understanding how this content relates to other things the students are studying. The skills of embedding that we also discuss in chapter 4 allow you to become comfortable sometimes following the lead of students and being confident that you can incorporate important and significant learnings.

Being well prepared means something very different from the traditional kinds of planning we have been taught. It means delving deeply into the substantive nature of the content, the significant patterns that are evident, and understanding how this content relates to other things the students are studying.

The issue of control in this type of learning environment is almost a nonissue. In fact, if you try to control, you will not only be frustrated; you will endanger the very learning conditions you seek to create. We do not mean that legitimate concerns of orderliness and self-monitoring are not necessary. They tend to be defined by the type of activity being used. In this way, the orderliness related to the needs of the task and the requirements of the environment can be taught explicitly and monitored with appropriate feedback and, yes, even consequences. Order in this case, however, is not something imposed by an external authority figure; it is an inherent condition of the activity itself and requires the necessary boundaries that allow it to occur. Orderliness also is conceived as a sense of overall coherence, which can help facilitate and sustain prolonged exploration into content, skills, ideas, and processes. You will be surprised how well students respond to this kind of order after they have had experience with it.

Complex systems tend to produce novel problems.

Real life is never free from difficulties. While creating these kinds of learning environments solves certain problems, it creates others that are often new and different from what we have encountered before. The emergence of new problems is another reason we establish process groups when a school is redefining itself and its learning environment. The opportunity to work through these problems as colleagues is not only helpful, it is a learning experience in itself. The school changes its organizational structure based on the new demands of its environment. It restructures naturally because it must—it is a dynamical, self-organizing system. We don't mean to suggest that this process of change is painless. It is, however, steady, incremental, and at times dramatic, and like all self-organizing systems, it needs periods of consolidation and refinement.

These same observations are true for the classroom. Orientation Three teachers have realized that perceiving the classroom in this way is an ongoing process of growth and insight. It spills over to our personal lives, our relationships with others, and our view of ourselves. In other words, there is no recipe. Orientation Three thinking doesn't just happen overnight, which is why in chapter 2 we refer to this book as a kind of "purposeful practice." Making this journey personal and professional actually lessens the anxiety about doing it "right." Each day creates new opportunities to learn. We never really "arrive." At some point, however, we stop and see how far we have come and how natural it has been, and we are amazed.

The ability to joyfully encounter the uncertain, to see beneath the ordinary, to perceive connections, and to respond with wonder and imagination are qualities that become valued and treasured.

Highly complex learning environments in contrast to more traditional classrooms require a greater degree of consolidation, or that aspect of active processing that emphasizes the synthesis of understandings and experiences. Using the terminology of brain-based instructional theory, most Orientation Two teachers already have some degree of skill in relaxed alertness and orchestrated immersion. Active processing, however, typically presents immense challenges. As we develop Orientation Three perspectives, however, we understand that active processing is a bridge that connects experience with learning, that challenges old assumptions, and that makes us more aware of how we think and what that means. Active processing means that we bring together the disparate learnings taking place so they can be organized into coherent and meaningful patterns. It means that we provide substantive ways for students to process and reflect on multiple facets of the learning process. In a variety of ways, students are asked to reflect on the content, the methods of inquiry, the connections to other subjects, their own feelings and thinking processes, the learning community, and so on. In short, they respond in significant and personal ways. Their responses become as much a part of the curriculum as what they have been studying. Again the skills of embedding become essential. The ability to joyfully encounter the uncertain, to see beneath the ordinary, to perceive connections, and to respond with wonder and imagination are qualities that become valued and treasured. Consolidation and active processing present the need to reconceptualize what curriculum is and how to think about it.

Permanent white water conditions feature events that are "messy and ill-structured."

So much for the five step plan—it doesn't work in highly self-organizing conditions! In saying this, we want to repeat again that a presentational format is highly useful and necessary when it is part of a larger picture of interaction and one of a variety of learning experiences. We hold to our view of things as "both-and," not "either-or." Having said this, we note that dynamical, self-organizing systems appear to have a life of their own. Scientists have often commented that even nonliving systems seem to be making decisions as they go. The learning event becomes a system with an almost distinctive personality. When one "event personality" interacts with other "event personalities," the systems merge in unpredictable ways. The principle that everything is connected to everything becomes an issue that places new demands on the teacher.

It is not that Orientation Three teachers do not plan. On the contrary, they tend to be extremely organized. But they realize that the traditional kind of planning is not that helpful. Certainly segments of time are necessary in a school setting, but the focus is not fragmented and lost in the presentation of individual and often unrelated lessons. Instead, these teachers tend to plan for contingencies, gather multiple resources, and in many cases work together to pool their talents. They often involve community agencies, do nonclassroom activities, and arrange for independent projects. They also create practice environments in which certain types of content can be individually assimilated or refined. These descriptions, by the way, apply to elementary and high school teachers.

One teacher we know developed her plans by sitting down after class and writing narrative reflections of what had happened, how students had responded, where she thought they were headed, and what they needed. This practice helped her consolidate her own complex experience and bring order to it. It was a personal use of active processing. She would make decisions based on these notes to herself and use them to prepare for the next day. On weekends, she would consider notes from the entire week and reflect specifically on the long-range direction her students were taking on the important lessons to be included during the next week. The principal also recognized the validity of this kind of planning and offered it to other teachers as an alternative way to plan.

Understanding dynamical, self-organizing systems helps us to prepare and work in a different kind of learning environment. But in order to do so, we must be willing to let go and be within the process itself, helping it to self-organize and reach a higher state of understanding. We have to realize that traditional notions of control are mostly irrelevant in these conditions and that a new way of perceiving what we do is required.

Letting Go

Letting go is almost contradictory to our common sense. Most of us have assumed that for something to happen we have to make it happen. We have heard that power comes from force, and it is the responsibility of those who have power to wield it with decisiveness and certainty. It has been ingrained into our psyche that letting go results in chaos and ultimate disaster. However, these ideas are part of a particular view of the world, so we see the world in the ways that confirm our beliefs about it. This worldview is the one of the machine metaphor. In a closed system, with little complexity coming from outside a tightly controlled set of circumstances, this view of the world works. Its practicality as a set of ideas is linked to its particular portrayal of the environment.

If we return to the metaphor of white water, however, and imagine being in a kayak in the middle of roaring rapids, we see that we don't try to control the rapids—we can't. Once we change the perspective, we also change the nature of what works and what doesn't. Although we can't control the rapids, what we can control is our response to the rapids—when to make quick, on-the-spot decisions, when to paddle forward quickly and when to back paddle and wait to be carried to the spot we have chosen. We may have tried to design our routes ahead of time, scoped out the boulders and the danger areas to avoid, but once we are there, the machine metaphor will not work. We let go of the need to control and trust in our abilities and skills to make the decisions that need to be made. Our survival may even depend on our ability to let go. We can't waste time complaining that we can't control the rapids.

In an interview, Shakespearean actor Kenneth Branaugh commented that in preparing for a performance, an actor works every line in multiple ways, trying first one approach, then another. He or she plays with the context over and over again until there is a match between the context and the way the lines are delivered. Next, Branaugh explains, an actor focuses on the mix of emotions and the interactions with other characters. Every possible contingency is explored. Then on the night of the performance, Branaugh insists, it is absolutely essential to "forget" everything he or she has learned and just "be" the character. The actor must have implicit trust and let go of everything that keeps him or her from being authentic in the moment. The actor has to be completely focused on what is happening on the stage. Such forgetting and being is what we mean when we talk about "letting go."

The Eastern view of the world has accommodated the notion of letting go much more than the Western. In a wonderful book called *Zen in the Art of Archery,* Eugen Herrigel (1989) writes a personal account of his process of learning archery. He moved to Japan from Europe where he would live and work for five years. What he learned about letting go challenged everything he had previously understood. It changed his life.

Early on, Herrigel's archery teacher told him, "the more obstinately you try to learn how to shoot the arrow for the sake of hitting the goal, the less you will succeed . . . " (30). Still Herrigel tried to shoot the arrow the only way he understood. He would use muscle power to pull back the bow, and holding his breath so as not to move, unleash the arrow. He did not see himself in relation to the event. He pushed forward, trying to force the arrow to do what he wanted. No success. Over and over again he failed. Again his teacher said to him, "Do you know why you cannot wait for the shot and why you get out of breath before it has come? The right shot at the right moment does not come because you do not let go of yourself. You do not wait for fulfillment; but brace yourself for failure" (31). The instructor's words still did not make sense. Herrigel was so goal oriented that he could not understand what it meant to wait. He focused so much on the target and his determination to succeed that he could not feel the tension in his own body and become relaxed enough for the arrow to leave his hand seamlessly. Gradually though, he learned. He realized that by letting go of yourself, you are able to be fully present in what is happening. You lose yourself in the event. You are the event. Herrigel grew in his understanding of what such letting go meant and was able to master the intricacies of his art. Finally, the day came for him to leave Japan. It was an emotional farewell. Over the course of his time studying archery, he had become a different person from the one he was when he began. His teacher cautioned him to be prepared that when he returned to his country, things would seem different: "You will see with other eyes and measure with other measures. It happens to all who are touched by the spirit of the art."

It is possible to learn to let go. What's more, it is necessary if we are to be effective in dynamical, self-organizing learning environments. The reenchantment of learning is about our journey to the place where we are touched by the spirit of our own possibilities.

Building Relationship

Control is not a dominant issue for Orientation Three teachers. Instead, they realize that an interactive environment that emphasizes connectedness and creativity needs a heightened sense of relationship. Whether from the point of view of a classroom or of a school, community becomes an essential issue of concern.

As we begin this discussion, let's consider how the new sciences might inform some fresh understandings and approaches to the topics of relationship and community. We know that all forms of matter seek to join together into relationships of some kind. Meg Wheatley and Myron Kellner-Rogers (1996) write

> **There is an innate striving in all forms of matter to organize into relationships. There is a great seeking for connections, a desire to organize into more complex systems that include more relationships, more variety. This desire is evident everywhere in the cosmos, at all levels of scale.**
>
> **Particles are attracted to other particles and so create atoms. Microbes combine with other microbes to create capacities for larger organisms. Stars, galaxies, and solar systems emerge from gaseous clouds that swirl into coherence, creating new forms of energy and matter. Humans reach out to one another and create families, tribes, and work organizations. (30)**

One of the first things we need to acknowledge is that we are always in relationship. Understanding this concept deeply, we can focus on how we are in relationship and the qualities of that experience that are most important. Again, as Wheatley and Kellner-Rogers write, "the webs of coevolution are so intimately intertwined that we cannot understand anything in its separateness" (29). In other words, the very fact that we *are* in relation to all things means that we are affected by everything around us and we affect everything, as well. Being conscious of this reality is a good place to begin any discussion of community. We have to realize that we are connected.

Communities, as systems, need a sense of purpose.

Any two or more systems come together for a reason, a purpose. In a classroom or school, the discussion of purpose can be a very clichéd discussion, or it can open us to the real possibilities of what being in relation to one another might mean. If we let the exigencies of the institution define our purpose, then we close our ears and minds to the individuals who comprise the community. If a single individual decides what the purpose is and negates others' voices, then there is only the assumption that there is a community.

One of the difficulties about creating school and classroom communities is that the people who are there often feel that they have no choice. They have to be there; they have to work, or they have to go to school. They really do not begin with any commonality of purpose. Unless the purpose becomes clear and there is an opportunity to bond in some meaningful way, community doesn't really happen. We have all had experiences with classes that just don't seem to gel. There doesn't seem to be any kind of sustained relationship that binds one person to another in a group. It is an empty and unfulfilling place to be. The only operating purpose seems to be "to get through it." On the other hand, when there is a coming together for a common purpose, the feeling is one of tremendous satisfaction. Communities need purpose and the ones who make up the community need to share in creating that purpose.

What often happens is that this discussion of purpose is treated as a one time discussion and then forgotten. We three are suggesting that identifying and focusing on purpose is an ongoing discussion. It is wrapped up in the reality of who we are and what we do. The three of us are codirectors, with our colleague Duncan Johnson, in a think tank organization called Gossamer Ridge International. We plan institutes that bring people together to share and extend what all of us are learning: how to facilitate the conditions that allow authentic learning organizations to emerge. We find ourselves constantly revisiting and reframing our purpose. It is amazing that each time we come back to the centrality of our purpose, each one of us is touched deeply inside. It has become part of who we are as a group and who we are as individuals. We place all the disparate things that must be done within the context of this purpose and almost magically it gives meaning to everything on our agenda. There is a coherence about what we do and how we operate that is deeply connected to the reason for our being together.

Developing a sense of purpose means focusing on the possibilities within the relationship. Can we use our being together to address our highest aspirations? Can we create a heightened awareness of possibility? Can we come to understand that we are not and cannot be separate, and that being responsible to others means that we are being responsible to ourselves? These are the kinds of considerations that are related to exploring and maintaining a sense of purpose.

Communities, as systems, need meaningful interaction.

Being in relation almost assumes interaction of some kind. The way systems self-organize is through interaction. It is amazing how many schools and classrooms want to build community but never have the opportunity to interact with their members other than in the defined context of a meeting or a presentation where someone in authority is in charge. Community cannot happen in this way. Purpose cannot be created this way.

There are different kinds of interactions that give us direction on how to apply these ideas in real, everyday situations. Some interactions are instrumental and procedural. For example, what is required when we operate as a small group and what is required when we function as a large one? What are considerations that need to govern what we do in formal settings as opposed to informal ones? These are merely pragmatic decisions that try to answer the question "What will make this particular kind of interaction work?" As teachers, we don't always have to lay down the law. Simply discussing the "rules" of the game works fine. When the "game" is over or the particular kind of interaction is completed and the setting is changed, then a different set of conditions may apply. This reexamination also gives us an opportunity to reflect on how we are relating to one another in various contexts and whether anything needs to change.

There are also interactions that deal with the larger issues of the community. These require a high degree of safety and trust. These kinds of interactions need to be inclusive and inviting. We particularly recommend our group process or some variation of it for these settings. We must accept the legitimacy of differing perspectives. We must also be open to having our assumptions challenged, not as a personal attack, but as a question to be considered. Once again, linking discussions about the community to our overall purpose keeps us focused on the larger issues of concern.

Interactions with others are inherently personal because they carry the assumptions and experiences that make us who we are. It is easy to sit beside people in class for a whole year, and even work with them, without ever knowing about them as individuals. We have had teachers who have worked together for years learn more about each other in a few moments of deep interaction than in all their previous time together. When we share our stories, we understand other people. Being able to share our stories and honor them brings a community together in trust and understanding. As we learn to accept our differences and celebrate our commonalities, nothing could be more important for a diverse, pluralistic society.

We three have observed that the quality of interactions varies a great deal in institutional settings. Allowing and encouraging honest, authentic feelings helps us as people move past misunderstandings or resentments. Most of us hate to deal with conflict. We avoid it at all costs and bury our resentments. Communities cannot be authentic without acknowledging conflict. We don't use "acknowledging conflict" to imply "fighting it out"; we mean committing ourselves to one another's well-being as well as our own. There will be some areas in which we cannot agree; our personal values will not let us compromise. How do we allow people to be their own persons and still be committed to them as part of the broader community? At what point does individual behavior become detrimental to the growth of others? Interactive, self-organizing communities make decisions about who they are and how they will "be" together, based on the respect, integrity, and commitment to one another's well-being. We are part of one another and cannot be otherwise. Systems cannot work against themselves and remain healthy. The same is true of communities.

Communities, as systems, help individuals find their niche.
Complex adaptive systems are characterized by opportunities for the various interacting elements to occupy a particular niche of their own that is useful to the entire system (Waldrop 1992). These interacting elements reduce competition and allow the system to build on the strengths of each of its elements. Cooperation and the constant process of giving and receiving are integral parts of system behavior. This process can teach us a great deal about building communities. Communities, like systems, require a substantial degree of diversity. Communities are not about conformity; they are about commonality of purpose and the reciprocal interactions of members toward their own benefit and the benefit of the whole.

This commonality of purpose suggests two things for the three of us. First, it is important to affirm the uniqueness of each individual and honor that uniqueness. It is necessary to help all members of a community find a place in which they can contribute individually and feel at home. Too often we overlook strengths that individuals bring because we look at the context too narrowly. It is vital for all members of a community to feel valued for who they are and for what they offer. There are times when members of a community have never even considered what their particular niche might be. They have been passive onlookers and have learned to perceive themselves as having nothing to offer. If we can turn that attitude around and provide ways in which every person has a valuable role to play, we will create a community with purpose and identity.

Second, in open systems we find that, as the demands of the context change, old niches become dysfunctional and new ones are required. Therefore, elements of complex adaptive systems need to be constantly open to their own growth and the need to assume various functions. While this need for openness is true in our classroom communities, it is perhaps even more true for schools as they seek to build a new culture. The old niches that people have inhabited for years and where they feel important and useful may not be there as the context changes. It is important to realize that it is the demands of the system that create niches and these change as the system changes. The feeling of displacement and uprooting are real and these individuals need help in seeing where they fit into a new culture. Everyone is important and everyone needs to feel a sense of unique contribution.

Communities, as systems, need a reflective process.

Systems have a variety of feedback processes that give them stability and provide information on how they are doing. For example, when we get a fever, our body is responding to information that tells it that increased body temperature is necessary to bring things back into balance. Fevers are nature's way of returning us to a balanced condition. Other types of feedback processes operate more openly with the environment and tend to amplify a system's response to positive conditions. These types of feedback assist the system in its own development.

The heart of our approach to change and community is the effective use of process groups. These provide opportunities for deep reflection, honest interaction, explorations of the purposes that are most meaningful to us and that allow us to follow our individual interests and talents. We can reflect on what is and is not working in our classrooms and schools. We can begin to examine our beliefs in terms of what we are learning. We can consider the nature of our interaction, and our levels of trust, conflict, and cooperation.

If you use cooperative learning, you know that just because you put students together in a group, you can't assume that they know how to work as a group. The same is true of a classroom or school community. Just being a group does not ensure community. Reflective processes provide ways to consider where you are going, what your purpose is, what you are learning, and how you can work together better. If a community is dedicated to its continuing development, these processes and questions are essential. Otherwise, the successes cannot be amplified into the system and used as a basis for further growth.

We have come full circle. Starting with an examination of our assumptions about the way we perceive learning and teaching, we began to look at what we do from the perspective of complex adaptive systems that are dynamical and self-organizing. When we understand our work from this perspective, we see that control is not the same kind of issue that it is in the machine paradigm. The need for relationship and community become more significant than does control as we prepare self-organizing, creative learning environments where potential and possibility for our students are expanded. Learning to let go and trust allows us to be part of the process we helped create. We can see the potential of the landscape of reenchantment.

Process and Reflections

Personal

1. Continue your journal of connectedness. Since beginning your journey with this book, have you noticed any significant changes in the ways you perceive your surroundings or the people in your surroundings?
2. Think about your own definition of *teacher* and how it may have changed over the years. Make a list of characteristics that you think are absolutely essential for teachers to have. Fill the page. Now categorize your list by grouping the characteristics into categories such as attitudes, skills, and so on, whatever makes sense to you. Now circle those characteristics in each category that you believe are most important. Finally, rank the circled characteristics in terms of their priority and significance to you. Quietly reflect on how you embody the circled characteristics in your teaching.
3. Consider the things you control in your classroom of which you are most reluctant to let go. In your own life. Briefly write about the fears behind that reluctance, and following the format of the daily list activity, respond spontaneously to yourself in third person. Do this activity with several of the items on your list that seem most significant.
4. Apply the systems characteristics of a community to yourself. In other words, identify an organization that you are a part of and explore your relationship to that organization in terms of an overarching sense of purpose, meaningful interaction, your niche within the organization, and opportunities you have to reflect and grow as an organization.
5. Reflect on how well you "walk your talk."

Group

1. Using your ordered sharing, share your reactions to the beliefs we say underlie all education ("Only experts create knowledge"; "Teachers deliver knowledge in the form of information"; "Children are graded

on how much of the information they have stored"). Discuss your reactions as a group. How do you see these beliefs embedded in your context? How do your own actions support or break away from these beliefs? What possibilities do you see?

2. Discuss what you think we mean by "dynamical knowledge." What do we mean when we say we must move to basic beliefs that reflect something like the following: "Dynamical knowledge requires individual meaning making based upon multiple sources of information"; "The role of educators is to facilitate the making of dynamical knowledge"; "Dynamical knowledge is revealed through real world performance"?
3. We have discussed aspects of orderly systems. Does it make sense to say that orderliness is different from order? How and where is this true? How do you collectively interpret orderliness? How would you begin to create orderliness in your school or working environment?
4. What is the difference between coherence and orderliness? Are they related?
5. Reflect on the people that you know who seem to connect to their students. How can you tell? What qualities do they have? Do orderliness and coherence play a part? In what ways?
6. Using the group process and ordered sharing, reflect on moments and activities in your life outside of school when you experienced a kind of "zone" or "flow"—when you were fully present in the moment to the point where there seemed as if there was no separation between you and the event. What were the qualities of that experience?

Teaching

1. You may use this activity with virtually any age group. Since it will appear on the surface to be unrelated to anything you are studying, introduce it as "a lesson in working together to create something that could not be created by ourselves." Organize in groups of three, or for very young children, use pairs. The gist of the activity is that the groups will create a story together beginning with "Once upon a time . . . " One person in the group begins the story, speaking *very* slowly—"Once Upon a Time There Was a Tiger." The other members of the group mimic the story as the leader is telling it. For this reason, the story must be told slowly and spontaneously. As you observe, you will not be able to tell who in the group is leading the story. After only a few moments (not too long) signal a change.

Without pausing, the person to the starter's left continues the story in midsentence. Again, the student speaks very slowly, with the others repeating as it is being told. Signal a change again; the process continues. You may quicken the intervals between your commands as the story proceeds around the group and let it go around the group several times. At some arbitrary point, signal a change that will end the story. Students may laugh as they try to keep up. You may have to remind them to speak more slowly. You may also observe a degree of frustration. Observe closely and afterward, help them process their experience. In other words, what happened? What did they feel? Did they have to let go of where they thought the story was going? This activity is an example of dynamical self-organization. Reflect on it and plan other short activities that allow you to experience and observe self-organization.

Universal Vision

7

The Reenchantment of *Content*

Expanding Our Cognitive Horizons

No man can fall
whose quickened dreams have sped
the edge of time
to follow the starpaths
of the gods—
the measure of his song
will know its birth
in timelessness—
and be of more than earth.

—**Stephanie Chase**

Seeing with new eyes, we can perceive the possibilities of an interconnected world. This new perception has implications for the learning environments we create, the communities we establish, and the relationships we build. It is a dynamic landscape requiring a deep understanding of process and the willingness to let go of our preconceptions and our need to control.

Reenchantment is that feeling of connectedness we experience as we participate in the creation of our selves and our community. It is experiencing the fullness of our humanity as creative agents in the world.

In our work with schools we have found a willingness on the part of many teachers to be open to new ways to approach their work. Some, in their own ways, have been teaching differently for years, although they could not tell you why or justify their practice in any convincing way. What we observed, however, was that a large number of teachers tend to put limitations on what can be learned, on the scope and substance of curriculum, and on the depth of interaction with it. Implicitly, this communicates to students to put a lid on their aspirations and dreams:

> **I wish I could still draw. When I was in grammar school I used to draw decently. I loved to draw in pencil and chalk. Art of all kinds intrigues me. I also love music, and painting, and carpentry, and metalwork, and dancing, and sewing, and embroidering. I want to dance in my own ballet class, play my clarinet, and draw thousands of pictures. Really good ones. Create beautiful poems, cook and sew for my children, decorate my home, have a good marriage, be an active volunteer, go to church, be an astrophysicist, go to Mars and understand all my questions about life. That's not too much to ask, is it?**
>
> **—Stephanie Pace Marshall, an 11 year old**

Is what the young girl wants too much to ask? And if not, how do we as educators assist her to realize her dreams? How we answer these questions depends, in part, on our "cognitive horizons"—the extent or boundary of our thinking and outlook. At issue is our capacity for possibility thinking and the extent to which we can enliven that capacity for and in our students. How can content become real in the lives of our students? What is the range and scope of the possibilities of which we can realistically conceive? And how do we expand beyond the limits of whatever we currently take for granted? This is what we mean by *cognitive horizons*.

A *horizon,* according to one definition in the World Book Dictionary (1979), is "the limit of one's thinking, experience, interest, or outlook." That is one aspect of what we mean by *cognitive horizon*. There is a dynamical aspect to this definition. That is, cognitive horizons are not fixed once and for all; the possibilities that we conceive change and develop and grow. They are dynamic and fluid throughout our lives.

In *Education on the Edge of Possibility,* Renate and Geoffrey suggest that irrespective of what we currently know, understand and can do, there is more. They argue that there are levels upon levels of development that lie untapped. We three agree with those who point out, for instance, that formal operational thinking is clearly not the final stage of intellectual development (Alexander and Langer 1990). There are vast possibilities for learning that we are only beginning to understand. At this stage of human history, the need to access these possibilities is greater than ever.

We do not wish to belabor this point. Suffice it to mention some of the avenues that await exploration as we all expand our cognitive horizons. These include alternative modes of thinking, including what is called *dialectical thinking* in its different guises, as well as an acceptance of paradox. It includes an awareness of the power of symbol, myth, metaphor, and narrative. It includes the joyful participation in possibility thinking and the celebration of human creativity. It includes, also, the examination of the new sciences with their emphasis on interconnectedness, wholeness, self-organization, and evolution. There is always more—more than we can conceive and more that we can expect our students to be able to accomplish.

Our task as educators is to come to terms with the reality of "the more," then to expand our horizons so that our students are better enabled to expand theirs. We do so by exploring some of the domains within which expansion is possible.

Facts and Concepts

As Renate and Geoffrey (1997) write in *Education on the Edge of Possibility,* many teachers simply do not have a grasp of the difference between facts and concepts. While some speak about the "concepts" being taught, even so-called "higher" concepts were often treated as bits of information to be memorized.

A *concept* is an underlying idea that gives a fact meaning. That many teachers did not understand this definition was actually quite shocking to us. The distinction between *fact* and *idea,* however, is absolutely fundamental. Indeed, it is only when the difference is understood that we are able to make the jump from teaching for memorization, which deals with facts, to assisting students to grasp concepts, which is the construction of meaning. We should add that even educators for whom this distinction is obvious often have difficulty in explaining the difference. They may grasp the distinction in their own lives and learning and yet ignore that difference in their instruction. We therefore suggest that the difference between facts and concepts be explored as a gateway into more sophisticated instruction. An ability to use concepts in mapping the experience brings the world of ideas and the world of experience together.

The reason this exploration is so important is that ideas act like interstate highways. We can travel great distances on them and intersect with other ideas from other disciplines. They carry us to places and "jumping off points" that we didn't even imagine. Ideas open us to expansion, to the "more" we did not know was there. They provide access to horizons of new possibility.

Subject Matter Craftship

To expand the horizons of possibility for our students requires us to be able to point out choices and directions that make their journey meaningful. Our own love of learning and mastery of our own craft can be an inspiration and a guide for others. Our experience suggests that all really good teachers are genuine masters in some aspect of what they teach. It is not possible to master everything, and in a dynamic and interconnected world, we often find ourselves swimming in the deep end of pools that are unfamiliar. Nevertheless, at the core of Orientation Three teaching is genuine excellence in some field.

Craftship goes beyond expertise in a subject or field because it includes the skill that comes from sustained application and experience. Craftsmen have a felt meaning for a subject or area. They grasp the patterns. They know how the skill or subject or discipline plays itself out in the world. In addition, they understand the personal work that is needed in developing craftship. To quote Garmston and Wellman (1995), "High-performing individuals and groups strive for mastery and improvement. They persevere to resolve differences between present and desired states. They create, hold, calibrate, and refine standards of excellence. They seek elegance. They strive for precision in language and thought. They know they can continually perfect their work and are willing to pursue ongoing learning" (6).

There is a story of a butcher who was known throughout the region as a master of his craft. A man of distinction heard of the butcher's reputation and went to visit him, to see if there was something to be learned from him. As he asked the butcher about his work, the butcher showed him the cleaver he used to cut up the meat. "This cleaver hasn't been sharpened for thirty years. Most butchers need to sharpen their tools constantly, but I have learned where to cut so precisely that it is like cutting air. I become so in tune with what I do that there is no distinction between myself and the work." The man of distinction left knowing that he had been in the presence of a special person.

When we participate in the ideas and understandings of a subject matter to the extent that they become a part of who we are, we are living our craft. In short, subject matter craftship provides indispensable grounding for the teacher. It is with this background that a teacher can know what students need to know, can empathize with student problems while urging them in the directions they need to go, can have high standards while being patient with the approximations and explorations that go into attaining excellence. To again quote Garmston and Wellman (1995), "Content knowledge is insufficient to ensure high-quality instruction. Knowledge of the deeper structure of the discipline is required. Teacher's manuals and inservice sessions on teaching strategies typically do not explore this territory. The critical arenas for exploration here are: What do experts currently believe is the most valid content in a particular field? How do they think about this field? What is the path from novice to expert thinking and action in this field?" (11).

Developing subject matter craftship helps us guide students to their own cognitive horizons. It behooves every person who wishes to be an Orientation Three teacher to be extremely proficient in some domain—to be a craftsperson with technical and scholastic knowledge and practical experience, to know how an idea plays itself out in the real world, to grasp the deep structure of a discipline. Craftship connects us to the joy and wonder of a discipline and allows us to be comfortable in the midst of process. We can share and lead and interject as the students need us.

A Sense of Purpose

Another essential characteristic of cognitive horizons is the ability to understand the relationship between purpose and learning. We can all suspend our need to know for a while, but eventually we need to see the reason behind something. In the case of our own interests, the need is already established and there is an intrinsic desire to understand, to know, to be able to do. Cognitive horizons suggest that we can see into the distance. In terms of learning, we can begin to see the possibilities.

Not all teachers perceive the relationships among interests, purpose, and learning. Or, if they do, they don't understand that these relationships apply to what they teach. "What they teach" is contained in a book or curriculum guide. It is separate from the students but somehow these students must know it anyway. It seems impossible to some teachers that students can learn the "stuff" and also tie it to individual interests and purposes. It does not occur to these teachers that what they are asking students to learn should really be richer, deeper, and more significant than is usually the case. Geoffrey and Renate describe this difference in *Unleashing the Power of Perceptual Change.* They point out distinctions among Orientation One, Two, and Three teachers.

Orientation One thinkers tend to ignore student purpose altogether. They follow their time table and lesson plans. This is illustrated by the sort of comment we mentioned earlier. "O.K. Now it's time for math. Open your books to page . . . "

Orientation Two thinkers try to both create and impose a purpose. They tend to do this by asking students to participate in well orchestrated activities with well planned and thought out questions and answers. There is also a genuine concern for other, less involved students, but it is of the form "this is important" or "you will need to know this at a later date." While they have genuine concern for the students, they tend to disregard the actual feelings and thoughts that students have about specific subjects and topics. This becomes a severe problem for more sophisticated Orientation Two thinkers. The reason is that they begin to want to work with the intrinsic motivation and real interests of students but do not know how to reconcile that with letting go of control and meeting curriculum mandates.

Orientation Three thinkers search continually for what appears to interest students and then seek to relate the curriculum to those interests. An example is a high school literature teacher in Australia who befriended some troubled adolescents in his class. After spending several weeks exploring personal issues such as family relationships and the problem of violence, he asked them if they might be interested in seeing how others have dealt with similar situations. This led easily into both history and literature, to the extent that many of these students actually became engaged in and excited by some Shakespearian plays and by the working out of the histories of the times covered in those plays.

These distinctions suggest a difference in "possibility thinking." Orientation Three teachers are able to see the relationships between students' interests and concerns and the substantive content of many different fields. They have a command of concepts as ideas and can see the concepts operating across disciplines, which gives them the ability to welcome student interests as an intrinsic foray into learning with purpose.

Meaning of Life

Great thinkers in every domain tend to do more than just follow an interest. They search for ultimate meaning and ultimate purpose. For example, Einstein was profoundly interested in the nature of reality itself. Maxwell (who developed the equations that prepared the ground for Einstein and others) explored the divide between religion and science with great passion. Deep questioning is essential to human experience.

Questioning deeply about what it all means is something that is not permitted too often in our society. There is almost an inherent discomfort that we will be face to face with our own unknowing. Our culture is one of answers and quick solutions. It is not uncommon, though, when Sam or Geoffrey teaches a philosophy course, for students to remark to them, "I thought I would hate this course and that the material would be dry and boring. But it was really exciting and has opened me up to a whole new world." Going deeply into meaningful questions does just that; it opens us to broader horizons of thought and action.

In a really impressive little book called *The Heart of Philosophy,* Jacob Needleman (1982) is straightforward in his claim that "man cannot live without philosophy" (3). As both a trained philosopher and clinical psychologist, Needleman does not mean this statement merely in figurative terms; he sees the need to go deeply into the meaning of our experience as an essential human need: "There is a yearning in the human heart that is nourished only by real philosophy and without this nourishment man dies as surely as if he were deprived of food or air . . . " (3).

Our culture has generally tended to solve its problems without experiencing its questions. That is our genius as a civilization, but it is also our pathology. Now the pathology is overtaking the genius, and people are beginning to sense this everywhere. "A geophysicist can tell us a great deal about the energy resources of the planet, but he can tell us nothing about man's proper relationship with the earth. A sociologist can tell us about the social patterns of crime, but he can tell us nothing about the real meaning of crime as a twisted aspect of man's longing for freedom" (7).

"Not things, but situations, comprise the world we live in, the world that faces us and claims to be real. The situations and problems of our everyday life, the crises, the ambiguities themselves . . . " (18).

For Needleman, real philosophy addresses the questions of everyday life that are rooted in the human experience. He states that "the function of philosophy in human life is to help man remember. It has no other task" (4). For the three of us, "remembering" is also the task of reenchantment—connecting deeply to who we are, to all things, to our own creative possibilities. As Needleman points out, the questions that lead to meaning are those that "touch the heart." They spark some longing inside of us that has been asleep. The power of exploring ideas lies not in the ideas themselves, but in the meaning when they awake the questions inside of us. "Behind the problem, lies the Question" (18).

Expanding cognitive horizons means that we lead students to consider questions rooted in their own experiences and help them to see relationships between the discovery of ideas and the discovery of themselves. It is a process of waking up the mind and the heart together so that our learning can be connected deeply to the meaning of our own experience.

Understanding How Things Relate

Have you ever observed a beautiful view from a high overlook? The landscape stretches out before you. You point out landmarks that you recognize and you see the relationship of one part of the land to another. You see other mountains in the distance and are amazed to be glancing over the tops of peak after peak. It is a feeling of exhilaration and awe. In much the same way, Orientation Three teachers lead their students to these cognitive vistas where they can point out the contours of the discipline, the relationships to other disciplines, and the far-reaching implications of what they are studying. Expanding cognitive horizons is helping our students understand how things relate.

Ellen, one of the teachers that we work with very closely, talks about her kindergarten through second-grade class, which had been building sixteen-foot whales in the classroom. One child wanted to build a dinosaur and Ellen said, "We're in the ocean now." The child said, "Well, I was watching the Discovery Channel and they said that dinosaurs were in the ocean and lived in the kelp." So the teacher asked for a plan. Sure enough, the child came back with a plan for building his dinosaur, and Ellen knew that she ought to give him permission to go ahead. She also knew that the whole class would get enthused. She knew that even though she did not like dinosaurs, that was the direction that the class would take.

Now how could Ellen have permitted this if it was not prescribed by the curriculum mandates? The answer is that she was working at several levels at once:

- She was interested in helping children become empowered and learn to plan their time, so she used this opportunity to introduce planning naturally.
- Writing and reading are at the core of her curriculum, so she could use a student's interest in order to encourage writing and reading without making them obligatory.
- She has a very big picture of how her curriculum will unfold over a two-year period so she can see how embarking on this project can lead into other topics that will be important.
- Ellen works beyond the level of facts and deals with concepts, and she knows how to weave important concepts into a wide range of topics.
- Ellen knows that important facts can be embedded in many topics and that facts tend to be remembered naturally when children are fully engaged.

We will explore some of the ways of thinking that allow her to operate in these ways. They are vital because one of the crucial abilities of Orientation Three teachers is the ability to see how things relate. This ability to see connectedness and the possibilities that lie in every experience distinguishes Orientation Three teachers from others. The Caines (1997b) write,

> Orientation One is at home with fragmentation and separation. It is taken for granted that subjects be taught separately, so that there may be 55 minutes for math followed by 55 minutes for social studies, for instance. Here, both the partitioning of time and curriculum are assumed to be natural and normal.
>
> Orientation Two thinkers appreciate some clear connections, but maintain some very strong conceptual boundaries. Links may be seen, for example, between math and physics and there may be acceptance of larger bundles of connectedness, as is becoming evident in some current approaches to the teaching of science generally. However, there are still some very strong conceptual boundaries between some subjects, so that the time spent in one domain (such as science) is not really seen to impinge on another domain (such as the language arts or literature) and hence to life where these domains often interact.
>
> Orientation Three thinkers have a sense of dynamic unity. Unity and wholeness can express itself in many ways. Orientation Three is essentially open to the multiple possibilities of interconnectedness. [These thinkers] know or sense that every subject in the curriculum is a way of organizing human experience and is therefore interconnected at a very deep level. Thus, they do not see the ideas in the curriculum as standing alone—they relate them to life experience . . . Ideas are seen as tools for understanding and making sense of life. Subjects and skills may have a basic focus, but every subject is connected in multiple ways to other subjects and skills at some level. It is this conscious grasp of interconnectedness that is at the heart of the capacity to integrate the curriculum and work with complex experiences.

Pinnacles

The air is thin at the pinnacles of great peaks
where snow lingers into summers day
and nests in fields like blanketed
meadows of flowers.

In endless procession, each peak gives
its own interpretation of grandeur,
each one shouts a whisper,
then joins its voice in a song
of empty space and roaring wind.

Their vision is greater than ours.
They listen to the voice of the sky,
the murmurs of the Earth's belly,
with a knowing that is beyond us,
and time that was spent living through
the generations of our infancy.

They are content to exist as they are
ever changing yet ever remaining the same.
Standing before the pinnacles,
we encounter their greatness
and for a moment share a common place.

—Sam Crowell

Creating a Sense of Direction

The content taught in schools mostly answers the questions "what" and "how." Educators spend enormous time and energy in these two dimensions of knowledge. We three have nothing against these categories, but in emphasizing them exclusively, educators may be missing an opportunity to move beyond them. Orientation Three thinking includes not only *what* and *how,* but also *where.* In other words, can we help our students gain a sense of direction for themselves and the society they will inhabit and cocreate? To help them in this way, we will need to transcend older categories that keep us and our students locked in to a worldview that is increasingly limited. The question of "where" brings us face to face with the new knowledge and new categories that we are coming to know.

Twentieth-century science effectively put an end to widespread modernist interpretations of our world. As modernism dies a slow death, there is uncertainty about its replacement. We hear the term *postmodern* a great deal from a great variety of disciplines, but for the most part, that philosophy has focused on the deconstruction of modernism, offering little to take its place. There is something happening, though, that gives the three of us great encouragement. People throughout the world, from a variety of disciplines, are developing understandings that may eventually help fill the void. Some (Griffin, Doll, Gablik, Crowell) call this "constructive or reconstructive postmodernism." The terms are not important. What is significant, however, is that the central motif of this work is the understanding and application of connectedness to the ways we think, the ways in which we build our institutions, the ways in which we live in relation to others, and ultimately the ways we view who we are.

We have already presented some of the principles of connectedness that, for us, provide a coherent bigger picture that helps transcend a fragmented and objectified notion of the world. These principles offer a sense of direction to the curriculum and to our perceptions of where to go with the knowledge we learn.

There are other voices that echo this direction. One of these voices is that of Fritjoff Capra. A quantum physicist, he has established the Center for Ecoliteracy to explore how the ideas of systems, especially ecological systems, can be used as a model for categories that help us reconsider our thinking about the world. His center has just collaborated with the California State Department of Education to design a framework for environmental literacy. The emphasis is not on facts about the environment, but rather the ideas behind ecological systems and how they reframe our understandings and perceptions. The draft framework emphasizes six major ideas.

Networks

This concept emphasizes the interconnected web of relationships that characterize an ecosystem. It includes notions of interdependence, diversity, and complexity. All are requirements of living systems.

Boundaries

This term refers to the scales and limits we find in nature. Systems nest within other systems and overlap constantly in various ways, yet still maintain boundaries and limits.

Cycles

Continuous interactions take place in nature that serve to exchange resources throughout the system. Cooperative partnerships exist everywhere for this purpose and all life changes in cyclic loops.

Flow-Through

This concept identifies the constant flowing of solar energy that sustains life, drives ecological cycles, and makes possible the food chain relationships that characterize nature.

Development

This term refers to the unfolding of life that is manifested in growth, succession, and coevolution. It involves the interplay of creativity and mutual adaptation that is necessary for coevolution to take place.

Dynamic Balance

The ways in which a system regulates itself through self-organization and fluctuation is contained in this concept.

On the surface, these ideas merely represent elements of complex adaptive systems as they relate specifically to ecosystems. Many of them we have introduced in our own discussion of systems. What we find hopeful is that if generalized and used metaphorically, these ideas can help us understand most things we learn, no matter what the subject, no matter what the grade level. They can be used to inform the way we organize our institutional cultures and the ways we think about issues within our society. In this way they, like the principles of connectedness, give some direction for how we can come to understand the world in a different way.

> ***Being able to see the what and the how in terms of the bigger picture gives us a sense of direction and a sense of connection to something larger than ourselves—life.***

Another voice that offers some insightful conclusions about the implications of the new sciences is that of Sally Goerner. In her remarkable book *Chaos and the Evolving Ecological Universe* (1994), Goerner summarizes characteristics that describe what this new knowledge and understanding might suggest. She bases these "conclusions" on an encyclopedic treatment of the new sciences and their application to human evolution. Again you will notice similarities in the worldview she describes and our own understanding of the bigger picture. The summaries that follow seek to describe characteristics of seemingly universal processes, which means they are happening everywhere in life. These processes are inherent in the world, but they may not be apparent, which suggests that they are also inherent in everything we teach and in the ways we learn. Being able to see the what and the how in terms of the bigger picture gives us a sense of direction and a sense of connection to something larger than ourselves—life. In reading these descriptions, use your imagination and connect them to the "whats" and "hows" of your work.

A Directed Creative Universe

According to what we know, the universe seems to be moving in a direction of creating increasingly complex forms. Everything in the universe is part of a creative drive. We are all part of a larger creative force that operates throughout the universe.

An Opportunistic Universe and a Cooperative One

Contrary to Darwinian thinking, the universe is opportunistic, not accidental. Cooperation exists alongside of competition and is a necessary aspect of being and becoming. Cooperation and partnership are new biological concepts that replace self-interest as the sole logic of life.

The One Is Many and the Many Are One

"All forms of being are part of one process . . . It is not just that living things are curiously interconnected; our interconnection and our existence, each and all, are part of an unfolding process which created us, directs us, and to which we contribute" (152). We are all part of the process, ironically unique, yet subsumed by a chain of being that will not end with us.

Constancy and Change

There is an interplay between a relative sense of constancy and change. Forms that survive are those that are able to accelerate themselves by learning, not by changing physical structures. Old models that depend on homeostasis cannot survive periods of accelerated change.

Necessity: The Importance of Being Inhomogeneous

Diversity is necessary for the growth and development of any system. Our differences can be the seeds of the emergence of new and critical forms.

Chance: Being Inhomogeneous Is Not Enough

Whether the seeds of new forms "take" is dependent on so many variables we can call it chance. But the seeds still must be sown.

History: Unpredictable, Idiosyncratic, Lawful

We know that the growth of complexity and the acceleration of the historical field are going to happen. We just don't know how or when. History seems to have a kind of logical unfolding, but not in a way that can be predicted or predetermined.

The Codetermined Universe

We participate in the process of change as we are also changed by the process. We are neither masters nor slaves, but in the large scale of things we have our place.

Demystifying and Reenchanting the World

"We are not a mystery apart from the world but part of the mystery of the world. The mystery is in us, of us, and more than us all at the same time" (154).

Cognitive Horizons as Vision

Cognitive horizons suggest that there is a bigger picture that relates the what and the how to a larger sense of direction. The where asks us to consider where this all fits in our human journey and in the role of our creative participation in the universe. The big picture indeed! When we combine a sense of direction with imagining the possible, we have all the makings for a creative vision. Margaret Wheatley (1992) describes vision as a "field." Using the new-science understanding of field theory, she suggests that a powerful vision can permeate an organization and have an effect on everything that is done. A vision can work almost like a magnet, drawing us ever closer to the creation of an emergent reality.

In our own experience with Dry Creek School, we found that the more the vision of where they were going was allowed to develop in the imagination of teachers, the more dramatic were the changes and the sense of purpose. In another example, Sam worked with teachers to help them create their own images of a teaching metaphor. Without any supervision or coaching in the traditional sense, these teachers all made changes based on their own reflections of the images they created. Educators usually think of vision as an organizational tool; its power can be equally apparent in classroom situations. We do not typically think of our roles, however, as visioning.

We three have described cognitive horizons metaphorically, as "seeing into the distance," "seeing the big picture," and as "possibility thinking." Each of these metaphors suggests that there is more to what educators are learning than meets the eye. There is something significant there that may not be immediately apparent, but it connects us to a set of events that is beyond our knowing, beyond our self-interest, beyond our sense of being individuals separate and isolated from the world. When we can see how what we teach relates to the larger events of the universe, we can be open to the possibilities of what that connection might mean in the world we help create.

Educators usually think of vision as an organizational tool; its power can be equally apparent in classroom situations.

There is a wonderful account of an Oglala Lakota holy man named Black Elk. The story was written by John Neilhardt (1979) after a series of interviews over many years. It is published as *Black Elk Speaks.* The central theme of the entire story revolves around a vision that Black Elk had when he was nine years old. Throughout his life, Black Elk keeps coming back to the power of his vision and what it meant. At first he saw the vision only in terms of his own people. Increasingly he understood that the vision could not be owned by a single culture; it was a vision of possibility for all peoples.

Author and anthropologist Joseph Campbell comments that Black Elk's vision holds promise as a symbolic myth for all of us. It speaks to the concerns of our world and the possibilities before us. Following is an excerpt from Black Elk's recounting of his vision:

> **Then I was standing on the highest mountain of them all, and round about beneath me was the whole hoop of the world. And while I stood there I saw more than I can tell and I understood more than I saw; for I was seeing in a sacred manner the shapes of all things in the spirit, and the shape of all shapes as they must live together like one being. And I saw that the sacred hoop of my people was one of many hoops that made one circle, wide as daylight and as starlight, and in the center grew one mighty flowering tree to shelter all the children of one mother and one father. And I saw that it was holy. (43)**

Cognitive horizons as a sense of vision means that we are able to look beyond ourselves and see the possibilities. It means letting the imagination of those possibilities pull us forward, into new definitions of our self. Visions are meant to be shared, to be opened to the community, to become part of a classroom culture. Black Elk states that "a man who has a vision is not able to use the power of it until after he has performed the vision on Earth for the people to see" (204). It is by sharing our visions that we begin to see beyond the horizon, beyond the self-imposed limitations that bind us.

Process and Reflections

Personal

1. Continue the journal of connectedness. Revisit the principles of connectedness presented in chapter 4. Consider how those principles, the ideas offered by Capra, and Goerner's statements relate to what you are perceiving and feeling as you write in your journal.
2. Identify a subject area that you really enjoy. Make a list of what it is that you truly like about this particular subject. In what ways do you continue to learn about it? Do you connect it in any way to your personal life and leisure activities? After thinking through these questions, make a plan for yourself to pursue more deeply your interest in this subject, just for the joy of it.
3. Think about some of the "big questions" of life that perhaps are under the surface. An example might be "In the larger scheme of things, why am I here?" or "What does it mean for me to create my life?" Choose a question that feels important to you. Find some quiet moments this week just to let the question be present in your mind.

Don't try to reason it out or come up with *the* answer. Just live with the question for a week. At the end of the week, reflect on the experience in writing.

Group

1. There are two discussions in this chapter in which distinctions are made among Orientation One, Two, and Three thinking. After you have done the ordered sharing, have an open discussion for about twenty minutes or so on your understanding and reactions to these distinctions. Hold pretty close to this time frame.
2. How do we make real the following sentence: "At issue is our capacity for possibility thinking and the extent to which we can enliven that capacity for and in our students"?
3. How does our ability to use concepts in mapping the world of experience bring the world of ideas and the world of experience together?
4. We suggest that it is critical for Orientation Three teachers to be extremely proficient in some domain—to be craftspeople with technical and scholastic knowledge and practical experience. We suggest that they "know how an idea plays itself out in the real world," and that they be able to grasp the deep structure and essential skills of a discipline. Can you see the benefits of their being able to know and do these things?
5. Discuss the following quotation: "Craftship connects us to the joy and wonder of a discipline and allows us to be comfortable in the midst of process. We can share and lead and interject as the students need us."
6. The real challenge of expanded cognitive horizons means that we "lead students to consider questions rooted in their own experience and help them to see relationships between the discovery of ideas and the discovery of themselves." Identify ways to teach this way.
7. We say that teaching for broader cognitive horizons is "a process of waking up the mind and the heart together so that our learning can be connected deeply to the meaning of our own experience." Please discuss this quotation.
8. Within your professional role, what are the areas of subjects or skills in which you really are proficient? We suggest that you list them, then take some time to reflect on them, using the following questions:

   What do you know?

   What really interests you about it?

   How can you or do you introduce your expertise into your teaching?

9. There are very simple practical indicators that tell you (or someone else) that this really is a field of relative expertise. The questions that lead you to these indicators follow:

   Can you talk about the subject at the drop of a hat?

   Can you solve problems as they spontaneously occur?

   Can you acquire new knowledge about the subject relatively easily?

10. Reflect on the occasions in your chosen field when you did the following:
    - Made detailed observations of what some expert was doing
    - Asked questions so that you could understand what someone was doing and why
    - Compared your current performance with your prior performance
    - Compared your performance with that of others
    - Tried out something new, and reflected on why it did or did not work
    - Agreed or disagreed with some comment or opinions expressed by others

    Can you see the above as a journey to greater cognitive horizons?

11. Consider the following questions as they relate to you in your chosen field:
    - How did you identify where to go next?
    - Did you ever aim too high? Too low? How could you tell? Did it matter?
    - Do you still ask questions about the meaning of life?
    - To what extent has your learning been driven by or organized around your deep questioning?
    - Did you ever ask these questions while you were at school? With what consequences?

    How can answering these questions help make your teaching and students' learning richer, more comprehensive, and more enjoyable; that is, how can answering the questions lead to dynamical knowledge?

12. Read Black Elk's vision aloud and, using the group process, consider what it means to you. When everyone has had a chance to comment, share any personal vision you have for the culmination of your work.

Teaching

1. Choose several concepts or big ideas that seem very significant to you in a subject you like. Consider the age of your students as you think about how you can help them to experience the meaning of the concept or idea rather than just to know the definition of it. Try out your thinking. Afterward, process the experience with your students, leading back to the definitional qualities or significance of the idea.
2. Introduce something you are about to teach by developing a focus question that has many possibilities. Try introducing this question with a story and using the story as a way into the content. Let the question guide your approach to the content.
3. Have a discussion with your students; ask them to personalize something you are studying in class. Extend their thinking gently without being didactic. Observe what happens and reflect on it.
4. Connect something that you teach to the principles of connectedness discussed in chapter 4, or to the categories offered by Capra or Goerner in this chapter. Is there a way to make the principles explicit in your teaching?

Circle of Life

8

Reenchantment as a *Source of Inner Knowing*

From External Authority to Self-Efficacy

> *We come back to where we started from*
> *and know ourselves for the first time.*
>
> —T. S. Eliot

As teachers become more and more comfortable with Orientation Three perspectives, they begin to see the world differently. What we have also observed is that they begin to view themselves differently, as well. We have found that one of the areas that seems to be particularly evident is having confidence in one's ability to move ahead, to take chances, and take responsibility. Such teachers seem to have an inner source of power that does not depend on the approval of others. We do not mean to suggest that they are insensitive or even bold. They merely do their work with a strong sense of commitment and integrity. They cannot do otherwise.

We have also found that Orientation Three teachers are effective in empowering their students in similar ways. Their students tend to be self-directed, goal oriented, and self-sufficient while seeing themselves clearly as part of a classroom community. This unusual combination is something that caught our attention as significant, as something to encourage. In this chapter we want to focus on what it means to find a source of power within ourselves.

The Source of Power to Act

We have observed that the source of power for many teachers is rooted in the external nature of the educational system. They rely largely on the authority of others, their positions, and the mandated curriculum. Power is perceived in external terms and one's relative position to these external forces determines what these teachers feel can or cannot be done. We have found, in fact, that there is often a discrepancy between what teachers think they are not allowed to do and the actual case. For example, many times teachers will tell us that they can't do such and such at their school. Or principals will tell us that the district won't allow something. Usually, not always, the principal or the district (whichever the case may be) is surprised that people feel unable to do something. What is often the case, however, is that the system works in a way that often makes doing something creative difficult. It isn't that creativity isn't allowed; it is that something has to be changed to allow it to happen smoothly.

Orientation Three teachers and administrators find their sense of power largely in themselves. They have an internalized sense of authority and believe in their own agency.

Orientation Three teachers and administrators find their sense of power largely in themselves. They have an internalized sense of authority and believe in their own agency. That is, they rely primarily on themselves and their own judgment based upon their experience and abilities. It isn't that they are combative; they simply find ways to do what they feel is in the best interest of the students or the school. In our words, they have a strong sense of self as demonstrated by a type of assertiveness. Gently or firmly, they tend to take the floor whether they are talking to school boards, with superintendents or parents. They tell their truth freely and listen carefully. They are deliberate in what they do and not indiscriminate; hence, they are respected and often consulted.

Orientation Three teachers feel empowered to explore their own contributions and determine their own paths. These persons feel free to deviate from any espoused thinking when it doesn't correspond with their own, intuitive truths. They more or less follow their own inner voices. They tend to do so, however, from the perspective of a coherent, well thought out, and credible theory of learning and practice.

Do you realize how significant this last point is? We are amazed that so many educators do not really know why they do what they do. There is a felt sense about it, but in our experience, it is rarely built on a solid, coherent theory of learning. We believe that this foundation may be the greatest single benefit of brain-based learning. Teachers come to understand their practice and have guiding principles to develop it continuously. Whatever the new technique that may be introduced, it is understood in terms of a coherent understanding of where it fits, which, by the way, makes Orientation Three teachers and administrators inherently powerful.

Orientation Three teachers have no trouble letting go of the system's domination over their own judgment and decision making. We do not mean to say they resist the advice of the system; they simply incorporate such advice as suggestions and check to see if these could enrich and empower their own thinking and their students' learning. Of course, the nature of the school and district make this easier or more difficult to do.

Although Orientation Three teachers are not oblivious to negativity around them, they tend to think in terms of possibility. They blend imagination with the pragmatic considerations of the situation. They are realistic and practical in what they set out to accomplish, but they keep alive a strong vision of possibility. In other words, they ask what they can do given the circumstances in which they find themselves. For these teachers, there is always another way, and obstacles are temporary boundaries. They are not put off by ambiguity and uncertainty.

Self-Efficacy in the Classroom

The collection of particular internal qualities that we have been describing is known as *self-efficacy*. Self-efficacy is largely concerned with the "exercise of personal agency" (Bandura 1992). It focuses literally on an individual's belief concerning who is in charge and who is making things happen. In our view, self-efficacy appears to be the personal quality that is the alternative to downshifting, which is explored later in the chapter.

Self-efficacy is important for at least two reasons. First, it is the quality that frees educators from many of the perceived constraints of the system. It is at the heart of their capacity to introduce new ideas, new methods, and new approaches with or without the support of the system. Orientation Three thinkers are high in self-efficacy and seem to handle change well because they appear to be able to suspend judgment more readily. In Ellen Langer's (1989) terms, they have fewer "category traps," which are more or less rigid beliefs that guide what they do in their moment-to-moment encounters with the dynamic world of the classroom and life. Second, in general it takes a teacher with self-efficacy to elicit a sense of self-efficacy in students: "The more effective person has a broader concept of self which is by no means restricted to his personal being, but which is also concerned with the welfare of others. As a consequence what he does to achieve personal adequacy contributes also to the adequacy of others" (Combs, Richards, and Richards 1988, 60).

The kinds of learning environments that support dynamical, self-organizing systems build upon the self-directed qualities that we are discussing. For both teachers and their students the following are some indicators of the level of self-efficacy in the classroom:

- Is there a focus on students' own decision making and the taking of responsibility and credit for their own innovations?
- In what ways do you foster independence through shared power and responsibility?
- Do you feel free to reinterpret or modify new methods and procedures based on the needs of your students and the context of the curriculum?

These qualities are ones that students will need in order to flourish in a complex society. They need to be self-starting and self-directed learners. They need to be able to persist with their own thinking in the face of pressure to conform. They need to believe in themselves and in their own abilities to master difficult material and solve complex problems. In short, they need to be empowered.

Students are not as likely to develop these qualities in a conformist learning atmosphere in which control is manifested in a delivery model of instruction, in which curriculum is mechanistically fragmented into bits of unrelated content, and in which the machine metaphor dominates the organizational structure of the school. We need to create environments that unleash the creative potential of students as well as of teachers.

The perception of power as an internal source for us to draw upon as we need it is a characteristic of reenchantment. Reenchantment is about our relationship with the world. We see ourselves not as separate, but as active agents whose consciousness and participation can make a difference. Research has shown that individuals with high self-efficacy tend to set higher goals and believe that they will succeed. They visualize success, while other visualize failure. Research also suggests that regardless of ability, individuals with self-efficacy tend to perform better than those with low self-efficacy, are quicker in discovering which strategies work, work harder, and have a more positive attitude. Bandura (1992) concludes that those with high self-efficacy can continue to do what needs to be done in spite of the pressures and disturbances around them. This is similar to a Chinese proverb: "The self-confident cannot be moved by censure or praise; the contented cannot be seduced by power or profit. Therefore, those who realize the true condition of essence do not strive for what essence can do nothing about."

Downshifting

We all feel the pressure of external events. And we all have felt those moments when we say in despair, "What's the use?" Not only do we feel this emotion individually, but very often we feel it collectively. Teachers experience the powerlessness to do anything about the conditions that characterize so many of our students' lives or the constantly changing expectations of "higher-ups." Administrators face the hopelessness of leading an organization that doesn't seem to want to go anywhere. Districts feel the frustration that on every side their hands seem to be tied by this group or that one, or by unreasonable regulations made by legislators with their own political agendas. External conditions do have power to affect our lives and the choices that seem available to us. It is easy to impose the same sort of power on our students. At every level there seems to be some unreasonable force that operates against good sense.

These kinds of conditions can lead us to "downshift." *Downshifting* is a psychophysiological response to the experience of threat related to a sense of helplessness or fatigue. People downshift when they feel helpless. Then they revert to early programming or instinctive behaviors and lose much of their capacity to think creatively or tolerate risk, uncertainty, and ambiguity. In effect, they experience the very opposite of self-efficacy. Thus, when a teacher uses power to force learning; when the students comply with the demands because they will receive rewards; and when such learning is independent of meaning, personal goals, or purposes then we actually induce helplessness and compliance—we create the conditions for downshifting. These conditions create within students a reaction against the forces that seem to control their lives and take away their voice. In the case of minorities and women, this feeling can be intense, as it may pervade every area of their lives. Even if we recognize these conditions, it is often difficult not to perpetuate them.

Part of the sense of helplessness is endemic to the system itself. If a complex adaptive system is not provided a dynamical, self-organizing context, then it will function in a stable state. Stable-state conditions can be positive in the sense that certain regulatory functions help to maintain the health of the system. But when these states keep it from responding to the obvious need for change, the very survival of the system is threatened. Stable state conditions create homeostasis. The homeostasis of an open system is its constant attempt to stay as it is. The system is highly resistant to change and as soon as something seems too different, it seems to scream out, "See I told you this is a stupid idea!" Just recall your last attempt to diet or to exercise regularly. Our physical systems want to maintain homeostasis or equilibrium. Therefore, we have a strong inclination not to change, even if we know that the change is necessary and good. Complex adaptive systems must be placed in emergent conditions of self-organization for change to occur. The flow of new information and new experience needs to provide the system with two important elements: alternatives and a coherent purpose. In classrooms or schools, downshifting can serve to keep us blind to new alternatives and assumptions, and locked in to the stable conditions that seem self-perpetuating and hopeless.

We three believe that the stable-state condition characterizes most of education today and prevents change from occurring even though almost everyone knows that it must. The assumptions on which education is based are growing more and more limited in their usefulness. Indeed, they work against the kinds of learning environments that can empower teachers and students to reach their own creative potentials. We need teachers and administrators with high self-efficacy who can work in spite of these conditions to create schools and classrooms reenchanted with the promise of possibility.

Following are some questions to ask yourself about the conditions in your environment and in your classroom that may contribute to downshifting:

- How do the goals and outcomes of instruction connect to what students already know or care about?
- How do you use external rewards and punishments?
- Are time lines restrictive or open ended?
- May students select projects that relate to their interests and goals?
- Is the curriculum mandated and controlled by others?

The helplessness caused by downshifting can be reduced by opportunities for choice, participation, and responsibility. Understanding that the tendency of any system to resist placing itself in situations of uncertainty and risk can help us move more confidently through those periods of doubt and disappointment. Drawing from an internal source of strength and power, we journey toward self-efficacy.

From Power to Empowerment

The shift from relying on the power invested in us by the system (and therefore deferring to it) to expanded self-efficacy and trust in ourselves is one of the most important transitions that an educator can make. In fact, this shift is at the heart of much of the transformational and growth process. (See, for instance, Barbara Larrivee, *Moving into Balance,* 1996).

Orientation Three teachers focus a lot of attention on their growth as people. The primary objective is a deeper awareness and sense of self. Embedded in the sense of self is a perception of the sort of professionals that they are. This contemplation of self and state of being does not begin or end with some specific event or occasion. Orientation Three thinkers begin to notice that everything we do is the proper object of our attention and awareness. They observe that everything is always in process. Their own words make this more apparent:

> **The process of self-discovery that we are all involved with is not a straight one nor are there steps that lead the way. There are ups and downs, ins and outs, frustrations and revelations. The key for my students and myself is self-reflection. We engage in thinking (not an easy step) about the "whys"and "because." In fact, I am sometimes referred to as the "why teacher." Before, I seldom stopped and pondered why, but now it is like eating and breathing; it is an integral part of my being a teacher and learner. Perhaps that statement is most important—my students and I are all teachers and learners together.**

The intent of this book has been to engage you in a journey of perceptual change. Both from our understandings of systems and from our research in schools and other settings, we perceive substantive change as an internal process. We all respond to as well as create the external events in our lives. The ways in which we perceive these events influence how we respond, and how we respond influences the events. And so it goes. Our map to "reenchantment" has been to empower ourselves and our students to see the world in connected ways, to look at ordinary events in the world as a source of joy and relation, to participate creatively and become part of the wonder of life, to learn to function effectively in the midst of process and change, and to see the intricate relationships and the expansive possibilities of knowing and being.

Our map to "reenchantment" has been to empower ourselves and our students to see the world in connected ways, to look at ordinary events in the world as a source of joy and relation, to participate creatively and become part of the wonder of life, to learn to function effectively in the midst of process and change, and to see the intricate relationships and the expansive possibilities of knowing and being.

Throughout this book we have mentioned process groups as a way to incorporate this change of perception into a school or institutional setting. Our suggestion doesn't mean that change happens overnight or always smoothly. What does occur, however, is a change that is deep and profound, specific to the context of the organization, and natural in terms of being internally chosen, not externally imposed. As we mentioned in the early chapters, it takes time and commitment to an ongoing practice of personal and organizational growth for real change to lead somewhere. Sometimes this change is gradual; other times it is dramatic. For example, several teachers we worked with told us that they really didn't realize how much they had grown until they went to some workshops. They said that they noticed that there was nothing in the classroom that held the information together, no theory of learning that made it meaningful. They found themselves being able to take away from the workshop useful information and put it into a broader context. Self-efficacy for many of the teachers has occurred through the group process. This process is not always easy or comfortable, but it can be a powerful pathway to growth.

If you have been doing the group activities, you have been using ordered sharing. We hope you have consulted the group process procedures in the appendix. If not, you may want to pay more attention to them at this point. We have found that the procedural process itself has power in it. Most groups eventually modify it to some degree, but the basic purpose and elements remain. Since process groups are at the heart of our approach to change, we want to expand on their relationship to self-efficacy and empowerment.

Understanding Group Process

We should acknowledge that there are many different and powerful types of reflective process. This section is not, therefore, to be regarded as an ultimate set of dos and don'ts. Rather, it is a process that is grounded in both theory and our experience. It is one of the ways we work with schools as they internalize new perceptions and understandings.

Our approach is to invite people to work individually and collectively at the same time. We always begin by setting up small groups with a sense of community, which facilitates the inquiry. We call these *process groups*, and they are dealt with in depth in our workbook *MindShifts* (1994). The purpose of *MindShifts* is to introduce more deeply the brain principles and the ideas that facilitate teaching for meaning. The book provides a coherent experience to schools who are restructuring. If you use the group process, you will see that over time the procedure helps to accomplish three goals:

1. It builds a sense of community in which participants can feel sufficiently safe to begin taking the sorts of risks that are at the heart of authentic, personal self-examination.
2. It introduces participants to the art of expressing opinions, even strong ones, without being attached to them. The letting go of attachment is absolutely vital for creating the inner space within which one can explore one's deepest beliefs.
3. It prepares one to listen to others without judging them. This listening has a twofold benefit. First, the less we judge others, the easier it is for them to feel safe and to begin to take risks openly. And second, as we practice listening to others at deep yet nonjudgmental levels, we begin to develop the art of listening to ourselves in the same way, which is how we begin to become aware of the thoughts behind the thoughts behind the thoughts—namely, the beliefs and assumptions that really drive us.

If you have not read the group process in the appendix, we invite you to do that *now*. The next few pages will be about using this process and ways to make it an effective and meaningful experience. There are some significant aspects of the group process that we want to point out. Note that the group setting is nonhierarchical, that there is no competition for time, and that a topic is selected that always allows for an unlimited number of opinions and that can never be exhausted. Note also that there is a deliberate and diligent attempt to remain open to anyone's opinion as having some possible personal meaning and relevance for others, no matter what that opinion might be. There is no discussion, nor is there interruption, so every person receives the full attention of the entire group. Finally, by avoiding discussion of the topic at the end of the sharing, we avoid a sort of subtle argument and confrontation from creeping in and having a chilling effect.

Much of the time that you spend in process groups will be devoted to the exploration of substantive ideas and to your own inner world. Thus, we suggest that you spend a few weeks functioning as a study group for the purpose of examining the material contained in this book.

In a formal study group, much of the energy of participants is devoted to understanding and exploring the ideas reflected by the words of the authors and the visual images of the artist. What we hope you will do is to examine these with a view to exploring your own beliefs and ideas. That is, you will use the book in order to come to know yourselves better. One skill that will benefit you and your colleagues in multiple ways is *active listening.*

Using Active Listening

There are many approaches to and descriptions of active listening, and over time we invite you to experiment with some of them at your leisure. A critical aspect in our process groups is for the people who are listening to be able to ask questions of the one who is sharing that will lead to further self-awareness.

Let us be clear about what active listening is *not*. It is *not* a way to challenge or call into question what a person believes. It is *not* a way to force a person to consider your opinion of what they are saying. It is *not* an opportunity to put someone down by revealing how intelligent or advanced *you* are.

Active listening is the art of helping another person elicit more and more of what underlies or what is at the heart of what they really believe. We suggest that you concentrate on two types of questions:

1. Reflect back what you think you heard.

The task here is to repeat in your own words what you think the person who was sharing was saying. Thus you give that person an opportunity to be exposed to their own ideas in a new format and to begin to see in how many ways an apparently simple idea can be construed.

For example, a person may say, "When I think of the notion that everything comes in layers, I think of computers and the fact that there is an operating system and then an application package, and that each package or program has a menu and that every menu has other menus. I sometimes think life is like that."

You may respond by saying, "What I hear you say is that everything in life seems to be constructed the way in which a computer is, with different layers of instructions and commands, and with some being deeper and more important than others. Is that what you meant?" Sharers are free to comment in any way they like: you may have construed what they said accurately from their point of view; you may have misinterpreted their intent entirely. Either way is fine, because what matters is that you are seeking to *understand* one another and yourselves.

Note that in addition to helping them clarify what they believe, you are practicing on yourself as well. You are working at listening closely. And while you are developing your listening ability, you are practicing articulating ideas to which you are not attached and in which you are not invested. After all, if they reject your interpretation of what they said, that is Okay! Behind the questions there is an attempt to understand and to support the growth of that individual.

2. Reflect back apparent deeper beliefs.

Every statement that a person makes, any idea that a person has, is actually built on deeper ideas. These are sometimes seen in what are called "hidden agendas," when a person is actually trying to accomplish something other than what is being said. We see hidden agendas in meetings where someone may want to manipulate a situation to gain some kind of personal advantage. We are not examining these kinds of hidden agendas, however. What we want to create is authenticity emerging as people connect, become safe, and master the art of self-examination.

At the heart of Orientation Three thinking is a philosophical perception that life and reality are essentially interconnected wholes.

When we three talk of deeper ideas, we are looking for something more than hidden agendas. We are looking for underlying fundamental beliefs that a person takes for granted and that act as a foundation for their other beliefs and practices. For example, when people use the metaphor of a computer to explain how the world works, do they mean that they believe in some sort of ultimate "programmer"? Do they mean that they believe that everything in the universe is like a machine? Do they mean that there is an underlying structure or form of which everything is a reflection? Have they thought about the spiritual implications of the metaphor? What does the metaphor mean in terms of how we relate to classroom practice?

You have an opportunity to begin to explore together some very deep and powerful philosophical ideas. This opportunity is absolutely crucial, because at the heart of Orientation Three thinking is a philosophical perception that life and reality are essentially interconnected wholes. The more awareness one has of what this philosophy means and how it works, the easier it becomes to integrate genuinely life into education, to connect subjects and domains with one another, and to create curriculum that students find personally important and meaningful. Thus, by means of the process, you develop your awareness in such a way that ultimately you become a more effective and powerful educator, but it is an indirect and nonlinear procedure.

The group process is designed to confront us with our own assumptions and purposes and to explore as a community where we are going. In a larger sense it is a way to focus on who we *are*. A way to extend this focus is to build it into other areas of our lives. Self-reference and reflection are ways to continuously focus on our own growth and transformation. As the Chinese proverb says, "If you want to know the world, look inside your heart."

Self-Reference as Reflective Intelligence

At the center of all learning is a very basic feedback loop. People do something, get feedback about what happened or how it worked, and that feedback provides them with an opportunity to make further decisions based on their evaluation of what happened and make further adaptations or appropriate changes. All learning, therefore, involves some opportunity for change.

Everyday self-reference is the ability to gain a general sense of how we function and what our own attributes and characteristics are. This type of processing engages what Gardner (1985) calls "intrapersonal intelligence." Perkins (1995) calls this "reflective intelligence." In his words, it involves "coming to know your way around decision making, problem solving, learning with understanding, and other important kinds of thinking . . . The stuff you get is very diverse—strategies, habits, beliefs, values and more—but it's all part of knowing your way around" (236). In short, reflective intelligence is the extent to which one knows oneself and one's own strengths and weaknesses. It is this type of intelligence that one finds in a vast number of self-help books on time management, decision making, improving relationships, becoming a better listener, and so on. An important aspect for educators is the extent to which we are aware of how we think.

Deep Awareness

There is a significantly deeper and more subtle type of awareness than what we call everyday self-reference. This awareness is important because it seems to the three of us that it is the deeper level that must be reached in order to effect the personal transformation that leads to profound perceptual shifts. The Caines (1997a) write extensively about this level of awareness. A label we can give to this deeper level of awareness is what Ellen Langer calls "mindfulness." She demonstrates through many different experiments that often we are anything but mindful, that at a very basic level, people do not think about what they are doing. It might be habit or automatic adjustments to routines or relationships, but our beliefs and set modes of perception become locked. She calls this "premature cognitive commitments."

Mindfulness means that we are present in the moment and that we pay attention to what is happening; it is almost a form of deep concentration. There is another element of mindfulness that is crucial for the three of us: it is being conscious of our own inner reactions. Self-reference is observing ourselves in the heart of the activity. Frequently, one of us may stop in the middle of a conversation and say, "Isn't that interesting; I'm feeling quite a lot of emotion as I say that. What's behind my strong feeling?" It is helpful to notice our reactions to things as they are happening. It gives insight into ourselves as well as to the situation.

Another kind of deep awareness is that of "living in the question," which is a way of keeping an open mind. It is a critical attribute for exploring diverse perspectives with others or for dealing openly with areas of conflict. Some guidelines that help to do this are offered by Isaacs (1993):

1. Suspend our assumptions and certainties. In other words, assume that you do *not* know.
2. Observe yourself "observing." Treat yourself as if you were a character in a novel whose actions you can see and whose thoughts you can read.
3. Listen to your listening. It is amazing how many tiny judgments flow through our minds as we listen and observe. It is fascinating to watch this part of ourselves. It's also a little disturbing.
4. Slow down the inquiry. Let your mind rest on a question that is important to you. Don't try to answer the question immediately, but ask yourself why the question is so important to you.
5. Be aware of thought. What previous connections are operating? To what experiences are you attaching the discussion?
6. Befriend polarization. Don't be afraid because there are various opinions and perspectives. Instead, see them as an opportunity for everyone to learn and grow. Move beyond conflicts about abstractions with stories that illustrate a different face.

When we let go of our certainties and the things we take for granted, we can view them in a new way. It is interesting to realize how many things there are we thought we believed, we really don't. We just haven't thought about them for a long time or had the input from various perspectives. It is amazing what a shallow basis most of the values we have taken for granted really have. It seems that somewhere in the past, based on something we don't remember, we decided that such and such was true and have just continued to believe it without really thinking about it. Deep awareness is important inside or outside the group process. We get to know ourselves perhaps for the first time.

Some Suggestions

The purpose of the group process is to create a coherent community of learners who are continuously growing individually and who, in turn, support the growth of others. This reminder is essential. It imbues the process with a power that is authentic, constructive, and serves the interests of everyone. As you use these forms of self-reference in the group process, there are some suggestions and cautions that are in order.

Be aware of the strength of emotional investment.

One key indicator that an assumption or deep belief or value has been engaged, even without our awareness, is the emotional intensity with which we respond to someone else's idea or action. Often we do not know what triggers our emotional reaction. Indeed, often we don't even know that we are being emotional. Thus, one avenue into ourselves can be gained from receiving feedback about the fact that we seem to feel strongly, which can cause us to be sensitive; each of us needs to feel the power of our emotions without lashing out. Because we believe something deeply does not mean it is something we should get rid of. Rather, the purpose of the group process is for people to become aware of assumptions that may have been hidden so they can be examined, retained, modified, strengthened, enriched, or let go. It is the unexamined life and the hidden assumptions that act as the barrier to our growth and development.

> *The purpose of the process is to create a coherent community of learners who are continuously growing individually and who, in turn, support the growth of others . . . It imbues the process with a power that is authentic, constructive, and serves the interests of everyone.*

Helping others see their emotional commitments takes sensitivity and practice. Ask permission to explore. For example, "I seem to hear a very strong belief or feeling in what you say. May I ask a question about what I hear?" Understand that people may feel obliged to say "yes" when they really don't want to answer any questions. People need to feel completely free to say "No, I don't feel like exploring that now."

Group process is *not* a therapy session; it is about understanding our beliefs and assumptions and how they affect our practice. It is also *not* a debate. *Do not press your point or try to prove that you are right.* Doing so will undermine the trust of the group. Most discussion groups people participate in are combative in the sense that they stake out a position and then defend it. If you find yourselves drifting into this kind of situation, someone needs to call a "process check" to bring the group to an awareness of what is happening.

Pausing to observe.

One of our problems as a society is that we feel overwhelmed by demands and rushed for time. Part of this circumstance is a consequence of what the world demands of us, and part of it is a consequence of our own learned and internalized attitudes. Some will find that it is incredibly difficult to be in a group where you can't "get down to business," "solve the issue at hand," or "make a decision and get on with it." We three have observed the initial impatience and discomfort of teachers and administrators who begin this process thinking it is a waste of time. It is actually a commentary on the kind of society we live in and how disconnected we are to the natural rhythms and flows of life. The three of us have also observed that when these same individuals allow themselves the luxury of meaningful discourse, they don't want to give it up. An absolutely fundamental requirement of inner learning is to give ourselves space and time to breathe and know that nothing *has* to be accomplished. The paradox is that out of this space and time of doing nothing will come greater accomplishment.

An absolutely fundamental requirement of inner learning is to give ourselves space and time to breathe and know that nothing has to be accomplished.

Several things help us adjust to this process. First, respecting the routines established in the initial part of the group meeting will assist you in developing a sense of orderliness. Second, practice taking deep breaths and having a moment of quiet before you begin, which helps to remove the pressures and activity of the day and helps you focus on a new occasion. Deep breathing is also a good way to begin any school meeting. It brings people together to focus on a common end.

Allow some time to consolidate your insights.

Use some of your group time for each person to reflect out loud a discovered awareness of one of his or her fundamental assumptions. During this kind of public reflection, it is not appropriate to interrupt, explain, or offer your observation about another person. It is vital that this time be one of personal reflection that others honor with absolute silence and permission. We are now creating the conditions in which we help one another to learn about ourselves. This experience is one of the powerful and most fragile experiences that we can have. Absolute trust is imperative and *casual discussions about others' responses when we are outside the group are unacceptable and against all rules of respect.* Honor others. Don't cheapen their insights for your own gratification. What we are participating in is the process of coming to know ourselves. As we do this in our groups, we connect with one another at deeper and deeper levels, and also become richer in our own being.

The Joy of Self-Discovery

Jacob Needleman (1982) writes, "Mind, real consciousness, is born in the confrontation between great reality and our present false condition; the confrontation of being and appearance, truth and inauthenticity . . . In front of real ideas I become still. I am in question; I am shocked by what I am and I feel the measure of what I am meant to be" (200). Our inner knowing leads us to greater degrees of self-efficacy, where we are less reliant on external authority and more able to realize the possibilities in front of us. We are free to act without downshifting. We have a coherent purpose that guides us and the collective efforts of the school community.

Though painful at times, self-referential learning is innately joyful.

This kind of learning becomes continuous and is not only a part of our professional identity but spills over into who we are as persons in the world—the ontology of being. Though painful at times, self-referential learning is innately joyful. There is something about the sheer joy of the learning that seems to us to be a characteristic of Orientation Three teachers. Psychologist Csikszentmihalyi describes it as "flow." Based on his extensive research, he has noted that flow "provides a sense of discovery, a creative feeling of transporting the person into a new reality. It pushes the person to higher levels of performance, and leads to previously undreamed of states of consciousness. In short, it transforms the self by making it more complex. In this growth of the self lies the key to flow activities" (74). Joy makes learning an end in itself. It does not have to be imposed or forced or externally motivated. The consequence is that our capacity to understand and perform at increasingly higher levels is natural and self-generating. We glimpse the possibility of the "reenchantment" of learning.

Process and Reflections

Personal

1. The thoughts we hold about things influence us physically. Try this experiment. Close your eyes for a moment and relax. Focus your attention on something positive and beautiful. Elaborate on the details of this image and hold it in your thoughts for a few moments. Next, create a negative image in your mind and focus on its details. Now switch back and forth between the two images about every five seconds, being aware of your body's reaction to each image. Finally, end on the positive image and sit quietly for a bit. Did you notice a heaviness in your body or similar reaction when you viewed the negative image? What was the positive image like? The ways in which we view the world affect us in more ways than we understand.
2. Make a list of situations in which you are closely enmeshed that make you feel "downshifted" or powerless. Rethink those situations in terms of an inner response that allows you to rely on your own sense of power. Follow some of your own suggestions.
3. Reflect on what you need from others in order to feel valued. Can you perceive yourself as valuable without depending on the recognition of others? What is it inside you that sustains you? What inner strengths do you draw upon daily that you may not always be aware of?
4. Choose something to act upon that is important to you. Follow through with it and afterward reflect on your feelings about yourself.
5. Reflect on how you may or may not empower others around you to realize more of their own inner resources. What do you do or not do that could either be strengthened or changed?
6. Reflect deeply on what *flow* means to you as Csikszentmihalyi defines it. Describe some times you experience this flow. What needs to be a part of your life for it to occur more often?

Group

1. Using your group process consider the effects of downshifting in your classroom and school. What are the conditions that make you feel powerless? Who decides how you must work as a professional?
2. Discuss in your group what it means to be a professional in terms of autonomy and responsibility. Based on your discussion, do you think teachers are treated as professionals? What would change if they were?

3. Using the group process, consider how you can empower students in the classroom. Be as specific as you can.
4. Based on the information about the group process in this chapter, reflect on your own group process over the previous weeks. How could you improve it? What have you learned? What is the nature of your community? Where do you want it to go?
5. Use the group process to delve even more deeply into your assumptions and into changes you would like to see at your school.

Teaching

1. Consider how your students could take more responsibility in the decisions made in the classroom. What would be a small step toward empowering them in this way?
2. What decisions about your classroom do you need to make to improve the learning experience of your students?
3. What are some of the restrictions you feel that may not really be there? What are you willing to risk?

Part 4

Charting Our Path

> *Orientation Three thinking . . . happens through a deliberate response to what we know and a willingness to look at ourselves, our schools, and our world with new eyes.*

Orientation Three thinking does not happen overnight. Nor does it result from reading a book. We know that. It happens through a deliberate response to what we know and a willingness to look at ourselves, our schools, and our world with new eyes. The journey to Orientation Three thinking is for all of us. None of us has all the answers. We can only seek to work within our own contexts and respond to what we know and learn. And, we hope, do so with others who have similar commitments.

Part 4 consolidates some of the general information shared throughout the book and puts it into perspective. In consolidating, we all face the challenge of "knowing." What will you do with your knowledge? How will you respond, given your own particular situation? This is the point where "knowing" and "being" merge—what we know becomes who we are when we respond actively in the world.

If you read this alone, you may not have engaged in the process reflections at the end of each chapter. We invite you to do so. We believe that they will assist you in consolidating the ideas presented here into your thinking and work. We also encourage you to use the book as a group process to engage your collective experiences, imaginations, and insights. It is in the creation of a dynamic learning community that the ideas presented here will have the most power and possibility.

Looking Within

9

Educating as if *the World Mattered*

> *. . . to surpass the given and look at things as if they could be otherwise.*
>
> —**Maxine Greene**
>
> *I will act as if what I do makes a difference.*
>
> —**William James**

We know that most education does not reflect the beliefs and practices we have shared with you in this book. The assumption that a teacher is one who delivers knowledge, who controls what and how knowledge is given, is very much alive in our classrooms and schools. There is an institutional infrastructure that maintains itself by implementing newer and newer ways of doing the same old thing. Our hope, of course, is that many who read this will respond to a sense within them that wants things to be better. In this last chapter we want to consolidate some of the major ideas in the book and begin weaving a tapestry of action that you may use to begin (or continue) your own journey. We also want to leave you with the idea that who you are and what you do matters. The same is true of your students. The visions, hopes, and dreams of each of us have ways of playing themselves out in the real world. A personal response to the learning occasion is the beginning of self-transformation.

Reconsidering Our Vision

Throughout this book we have tried to convey that reenchantment is not something foreign to us, but rather it is a natural part of our heritage as humans. Indeed the distinction between disenchantment and reenchantment is that we have "forgotten" or become separated from a heritage of connection, wonder, and joy. Some may argue that this is a heritage of ideals, not reality, and they may be right. It is also true, however, that connectedness, wonder, and joy are woven into the fabric of human experience for all of us, yet seldom do we integrate their potential and power into our lives. The affirmation of this heritage has been replaced by a technical approach to living that manipulates the world as if it were made of objects that fit into a broader machinelike picture. Our institutions, assumptions, and perceptions are oriented to this worldview.

> *Connectedness, wonder, and joy are woven into the fabric of human experience for all of us, yet seldom do we integrate their potential and power into our lives.*

We three are not advocating a return to some primitive, romanticized state that ignores the conditions and circumstances of the present world. We are pointing to the fact that the view of ourselves as removed and separate from one another, from the Earth, from the events and circumstances of our lives is *not* an accurate perception of the world in terms of the new sciences of our day. The paradox of this condition is that it returns us to the roots of our humanity while it propels us forward to a yet-to-be-realized future. Reclaiming a sense of ourselves that perceives its broader connections seems absolutely essential if we are to venture into the uncharted landscape of a new paradigm. At the heart of this picture of reality is the self-referential relationship between inner and outer states of being.

We believe that who people are and the assumptions that are manifested in their practice matter. How educators create classroom and organizational environments and for what purposes matter. The processes that allow us to relate to one another, make decisions, and support one another's growth matter. One of the central questions that drives us is how to create the conditions that allow us to transcend our limited perspective

The Dream

The Dream reaches beyond me
to embrace the possibility of distant recollections—
just out of reach from memory,
just far enough for me to know
that I do not know;
like dry sap trying to remember
its runny ooze,
like a forest trying to remember
the open meadow.

The Dream knows itself
in pure imagination.
It waits to be discovered,
lingering in cloud puffs
on a warm, sunny day,
or in the gurgling, rushing sounds
of melting snows during spring.

The Dream is the yet to be,
that already is—
a memory waiting to be born
in a different place and time,
an enchanted reminiscence
of who we are.

—Sam Crowell

of possibility. How can we creatively participate, each in our own individual ways, in unleashing the power of a new way of thinking and living?

This book has been about making a transition to become Orientation Three teachers. Without the perceptual understanding of this kind of thinking, advanced instructional approaches are likely not to be effective, or if they are, will only serve to perpetuate an understanding of the world that continues to distance us from ourselves and the environment.

Each of us is a system. We live in these systems; we are part of them. Simply understanding ourselves as a system, however, does not move us out of a mechanistic way of viewing the world. In fact, our machines have now become systems, as well. The computer world is the new reality of our time. How can we implement a practice that affirms and celebrates a reenchanted sense of our humanity and also accentuates an understanding of ourselves and our organizations as complex adaptive systems? How can we expand a philosophical materialism that only legitimatizes physical reality to include questions that investigate nonmaterial possibilities? How do we rethink our political, social, and economic structures to address an extended view of our relationships and responsibilities? How do we learn to see ourselves as part of the natural systems of Earth and understand that we are not separate from this "Earth family" with which we share life? This is the reconstructive project of our historical moment.

Owning What We Know

A crucial point of reenchantment is that we cannot separate ourselves from our knowing. Whether it is we or our students, knowing calls us into action. The individual question for each of us no matter what we learn is "How will I respond?" Sam has called this "responsive learning," that is, learning that calls us forth into the world. In this chapter we want to explore where to go with the understandings this book has highlighted. How will we respond to our own learning?

From the new sciences we learn that the world is inherently connected, relational, and creative. It is composed of wholes within wholes within wholes—layers of recursive patterns that repeat themselves into infinity. We learn that nothing in the world is static or stationary; rather, all things are swirls of moving energy—light and sound—that somehow organize around a kind of purpose and meaning, scientifically called *teleonomy.* These "things" function in relation to other "things," creating systems within systems that grow in complexity and interdependence.

A web of relationships and interconnected systems characterize everything. Open systems are dynamic and self-organizing, and they function to perpetuate themselves and change at the same time. As complexity grows within their environment, the need to change becomes more and more essential, which means that all systems are enmeshed in process and possibility. To the degree that a system establishes connective relationships, it expands its own ability (for it is not and cannot be separated from its relationships). We also know that a system develops over time, sometimes slowly and sometimes with punctuated leaps. Each new development requires consolidation, refinement, and the creation of new skills. Each new development is a creative act.

From the new sciences we learn that the world is inherently connected, relational, and creative. It is composed of wholes within wholes within wholes—layers of recursive patterns that repeat themselves into infinity.

If we are each a complex, adaptive system; if every one of our schools and classrooms functions as a dynamical, self-organizing system; if we understand ourselves in terms of our connectedness, the quantum nature of our nonseparation and the holographic aspects of our wholeness; if we acknowledge our innate creative capacities for expression and participation; then what will we do with this knowledge? How will we respond in our personal lives? As teachers and administrators? As schools and districts? Dynamical knowledge calls our "beingness" into question. In other words, dynamical knowledge becomes integrated into our lives as felt meaning. It is at this point that we are no longer addressing what we know, but who we are. Dynamical knowledge brings us to the point of responsive learning.

Walking the Road We Create

One of the things the three of us learned early on in working with schools is that every school is a unique set of circumstances and that what works in one school does not always work in another. We have found, however, that if schools and other organizations engage in an authentic kind of group process that allows and supports one another's growth and exploration, things happen. Creative action is generated. In addition, if the group process is focused around a coherent set of ideas, then the action has more sustained purpose and is not as disruptive or unnatural to the perceived needs of the group.

In this new landscape of ideas, we know that certain processes will create action, but the results of the action are dependent on each context and the variables of the system itself. If change is centered around a coherent set of ideas, then those ideas can be used to guide the process. If change is merely throwing the system into disequilibrium, then probably a set of guiding principles will need to emerge. Ongoing self-reflection is a fundamental requirement for a system in transition. Learning about our learning is a key factor in walking an uncharted path. The process is immensely invigorating and satisfying, but it is not easy.

Gregory Bateson's research with dolphins and porpoises tells a fascinating and important story. The story provides insight into our own personal and organizational learning. First, the trainer taught the porpoise to do tricks, such as flips and somersaults, by rewarding it with a fish every time the animal did the trick successfully. As the porpoise learned new tricks, the trainer changed the reward schedule to every three tricks. The researchers then decided to reward the porpoise only after it invented a new trick. What happened was interesting. At first, the porpoise went through a three-trick pattern. It repeated the three tricks and showed frustration and anger when it wasn't rewarded. Then it went through the entire repertoire of tricks, still not receiving any reward. It exhibited signs of furious anger and pain, seemingly confused and frustrated. It performed the same tricks over and over again, but to no avail. What happened next surprised everyone. The porpoise's attitude suddenly changed from being angry and frustrated to realizing that it did not have to be stuck in its old patterns of learning. It then created and performed a brand new trick. It subsequently performed four additional new stunts that had never before been observed in its species! As Berman (1981), who reports this story, comments, "The porpoise became trans-contextual" (231), which means that it was able to see itself within the limitations of its context and go beyond those limitations.

It is this leap of understanding that defines Orientation Three thinking. Yes, it can be frustrating, perhaps even painful, but we free ourselves to move forward in a new and creative relationship with the world. Bateson observed that the true purpose of education is an "awakening to ecstasy." For the three of us, this awakening means the reenchantment of learning. Can we as educators see ourselves thinking within our own paradigm and move beyond it to create possibility within the world?

Mapping Our Journey

This issue is not just an educational one. As we have noted, it encompasses every institution in society. How do we start? When we journey into an uncharted landscape where do we go and what do we do? Kevin Kelly (1994) offers nine observations of how nature is inherently creative and self-organizing. We elaborate on these observations to address considerations you may need addressed before you begin your journey. These observations or principles say in a different way many things that we have discussed in this book. Using different language sometimes helps provide an additional "take" on how to map our journey. Like many of our own observations, these come out of the knowledge of biological evolution and the science of complexity.

1. Distribute Being

Distribution of being is described as "the spirit of the beehive." The functions and thinking of any complex system need to be distributed to smaller units that are working for a larger common purpose. Even these distributed units may also be distributed. One principle of connectedness that illustrates this is *the whole is greater than the sum of its parts.* In other words, the interaction of the whole creates "something out of nothing." Life, intelligence, and evolution all begin in distributed systems.

What distribution of being means in terms of schools and classrooms is that individuals need to feel a part of something and need opportunities to participate in roles and responsibilities that everyone deems valuable. Rather than having one person make all the decisions, responsibility is distributed and coordinated. The entire system benefits when creative energy extends to all parts of the system. Teachers can create more complex environments that are simple in design and function. The key is that individuals, students or teachers, feel a part of something larger than themselves.

2. Control from the Bottom Up

In a distributed system everything happens at once. The problems and situations are wide and fast moving. They defy the attention of any central authority and must be handled by those units closest to the problem. In this way, problems remain in their simplest form. The larger system then must respond to or modify the decision based on the overall good of the whole.

A school might need to organize itself in smaller communities in which decisions can be made quickly and efficiently and in which students can receive the most direct services available. While specialization can be helpful and inform the decisions, centralized specialization only serves to limit both the service and the response time. Rather than abdicate responsibility when decisions need to be made, there needs to be the freedom to act as conscientiously as possible at the level of need.

In classrooms, this same understanding can be used to create situations of responsibility and empowerment to make decisions. Even kindergarten children can be entrusted with appropriate kinds of decisions in which they are guided to make choices, understand consequences, and have responsibilities. One of the first things some of our Orientation Three kindergarten teachers did to modify their classrooms was to put materials at an accessible level so students could get them whenever they needed them. This one action saved the teachers countless requests and steps. It made the children feel worthy of deciding for themselves. Cooperative learning also provides opportunities for responsibility and decisions. Older students begin to make all kinds of decisions that are part of a complex yet organized environment. We three are advocates of well-designed apprenticeship programs through which students encounter decision-making opportunities and responsibility in the real world.

Simple ground rules dealing with consideration, boundaries, safety, and process are usually sufficient to guide complexity. Ironically, complexity is usually guided by very simple rules. This principle is important to remember. Activities and problems present opportunities to revisit or reconsider the values or ideas that guide us. In either case, the decisions at smaller levels need to be seen periodically in relation to the larger system's values and concerns. Whether in a school organization or a classroom, decision making can be adjusted to include the genuine participation and authority of each person.

3. Cultivate Increasing Returns

Whatever is cultivated increases, whether it is confidence, success, learning, or integrity. In terms of systems, something in the environment is altered so that it can be increased. This law works throughout the sciences. If we become aware of those things we cultivate, we can participate more consciously in creation. This awareness applies also to thoughts, ideas, and emotions.

Whatever is cultivated increases, whether it is confidence, success, learning, or integrity.

One of the real pleasures of working with Orientation Three teachers is the degree to which they cultivate in their students an eagerness to learn, which is especially apparent in their own lives. It is also evident in their classrooms, where their students work at high conceptual levels, investigate provocative questions, and master skills above grade expectations. It is equally impressive at the school level where teachers genuinely respond to their own learning with imagination and creative new ideas. No one told them to be creative; it is just the way they learn to operate.

4. Grow by Chunking

Creating complex systems that work takes time. Each independent system must grow and develop incrementally, adding to the overall complexity of the system. Just as a forest begins in a meadow and develops over time, so do organizations, which is why we begin with process groups and allow growth that is unique to each organization and environment.

Growth and development do not happen evenly or on a schedule. The influences of various contexts and conditions are constant and fluctuating. Most approaches to instructional innovations, curricular change, and reorganization seem to assume that inner growth is not necessary. So we have innovations that are misused or misunderstood, we have curriculum that is viewed as "one more thing on top of everything else," and we have new department names or a new school theme or a consolidation of administrative roles that are meant to solve old problems in new ways.

For the three of us, the group process creates conditions whereby sustained and relevant development can occur. Our vision of school restructuring is that, as the growth of individuals takes place, understandings emerge that need to be supported in tangible ways. The dreams and aspirations of staff are honored and allowed to blossom, given the constraints of the system and the obstacles that need to be collectively addressed. Organizational change is guided by understandings about systems themselves, but also by the creative energy of everyone participating. Risks are supported. Responsibilities are distributed. Control is also distributed to those making decisions. The larger focus of the system is guided by principles of connectedness and an operational understanding of learning based on the brain. Emphasis on the bigger picture stretches the school into greater depth and substance, with the larger issues of purpose and meaning clearly guiding the school to consider the significant themes of human relatedness.

There are downs in this process, as well. Conflicts, moving ahead too quickly or too slowly, lack of consolidation of growth and change, political pitfalls, and disingenuous commitments are some of the many. But these problems occur no matter what kind of change is attempted. The point here is that effective group process allows a faculty and staff a chance to encounter these challenges in an ongoing way, to be clear about their commitments, and to assist others who join the organization to understand what is happening.

Growth takes time and commitment to an ongoing practice. Such is the premise of this book. It is meant to be a start of a practice that can be revisited, reaffirmed, and understood in deeper and more substantive ways.

5. Maximize the Fringes

Diversity is a requirement of complex systems that are able to adapt to changes in the environment. In natural systems, adaptations happen nearest the borders or in isolated clusters. Innovations keep alive the growth of the entire system. Increasing the fringes along borders allows a greater infusion of new ideas, which can then be consolidated by the larger system.

If there is a commitment ahead of time to this idea, it may help schools and other organizations deal with the inevitable strain that innovation places on the old system. There will be those who move ahead quickly and those who will take longer to unlearn previous ways of thinking or adapt to new skills and practice. Each of these can be honored, for one creates an impetus to change and the other places a natural constraint on the growth of the system. There needs to be a dynamic relationship between the two, however, where those holding back perceive the need to move progressively ahead and those moving ahead understand the need for the entire system to modify itself without force. The fringes will arrive at system limitations first and there will be a need to address these concerns in a way that leads everyone forward. These natural system junctures will need to happen. It will seem like something is stopped up, and once the stoppage is cleared, everything flows again, at least until the next time.

6. Honor Your Errors

The process of creation happens as much by surprise as it does by design. Some of the most beautiful art pieces are the results of "accidents" that were noticed and used to create something out of the ordinary. The same is true in nature. When we treat everything as possibility, we find there is always more than meets the eye. An organization needs an atmosphere where positive errors can be explored for their possibility.

This atmosphere is so necessary in classrooms and schools. We need space to solve the problems we create. We did not learn to walk by not falling down or to talk without testing a variety of sounds and pronunciations. Our errors actually provide us opportunities to see how things might work. At times these errors are more valuable than things that do work because when things work we often don't look any further for other possibilities. We three have known many who refuse to try anything different because what they do "works." They often have a limited perspective of what exactly is working, but they are nonetheless dissuaded from anything that might place them in a position of not doing something "right."

Mapping a journey to a new landscape of ideas and a new education requires us to have patience with ourselves and with one another. It cannot be a blaming game where we point fingers and make accusations. Rather, we encounter one another with truthfulness and with the expectation that problems can be solved. Within process groups we must encounter our own disappointments and errors as opportunities to lead others around our pitfalls. We must also encounter conflicts and misunderstandings as opportunities to solidify a collective purpose.

7. Pursue No Optima—Have Multiple Goals

The process of learning and developing in a complex system means that nothing ever works perfectly. There are too many things happening that, at different times, need attention and resources. Being ever-changing means that larger purposes are pursued in multiple ways. This fact does not, however, negate the importance of coherence within the system.

When control and authority are distributed within a system, multiple goals emerge. The goals may be based on individual interests or inclinations; they may pertain to specific functions that require attention and focus. What is important is that the system as a whole is informed by what is happening. The flow of information can be an enormous issue. The purpose of information in this context, however, is not just to inform; it is to help the system itself learn. We don't often think about a classroom or school as a living system, but in many ways it functions just as an organism functions, and we are conscious parts of its being. Therefore a classroom or school "learns" in much the same way we do—by making sense of experience and reflecting on how experience helps it to fulfill its purpose.

By being conscious that we are dynamic parts of larger systems, we can both affirm our individuality and see ourselves in relation to something larger. The principle of connectedness that characterizes this interrelationship is "every whole is part of a greater whole." When we perceive ourselves in relation to larger and larger wholes, we can begin to perceive the inherent power of that condition. We are part of everything.

8. Seek Persistent Disequilibrium

If a system reaches equilibrium, it dies. On the other hand, as we discussed in chapter 6, if there is too much disequilibrium, the system explodes. Maintaining a dynamic balance between these two extremes is the constant challenge of all complex adaptive systems. We three believe that group process and consistent reflection best enable systems to respond to this challenge.

The new sciences tell us that there is only process. Substance and materiality emerge from the dynamism of energy and process. As philosopher Richard Rorty notes, we must "keep the conversation going" (in Doll 1993, 151) We know from Piaget's and others' work that disequilibrium is essential for learning. Experiential learning models emphasize dissonance and challenge. To transform experience into learning, however, requires a way to process the experience. For a school to engage in a concerted effort of change and not set in motion a process that allows it to learn from its collective experience and to actively engage itself in new possibilities is to undermine its own attempts. Everything we know about learning and everything we know about systems points to the need to process experience in deep and substantive ways. Whether you call them reflective, dialogue, discourse, or process groups is not the critical point. Some process is necessary for growth and learning to occur.

Whether it is in a classroom or a school, active processing of complex experience lets learning emerge out of its own context and allows it to be shared with those educators who hold a common purpose. It is in this kind of environment that real learning occurs.

9. Change Transforms Itself

Change is structured when it is coordinated. Our premise is that schools *must* change. There is no other option in a complex world. If they do not change, they will die. We believe that by learning to live and be creative in a systematic world, we can coordinate the change. We must become part of the change. When we see ourselves in this way, we understand that change is both internal and external. By engaging in a practice of seeing the world with new eyes and approaching the world we see as an integral part of it, we move toward self-transformation.

By engaging in a practice of seeing the world with new eyes and approaching the world we see as an integral part of it, we move toward self-transformation.

Beginning the Journey

It is interesting to us that many who write of systems still focus most or all of their attention on external relationships and ignore the internal changes and processes that occur as a system becomes different. This refusal to deal with inner processes is not only suspect in terms of the scientific evidence to the contrary, it is an indication of a philosophical mindset that remains caught in a modernist materialism. These writers present only half the picture. The principle of connectedness that seems most relevant to us here is that "inner and outer reflect each other." There is a dynamism that is engaged as systems, human or nonhuman, reorganize themselves. It is not until the system dynamically reaches critical stages in terms of its reevaluation that movement toward change begins.

Just think about your personal life. We make changes all the time based on circumstances and situations. Most often, however, these changes are temporary adaptations that do not last long. The real, substantive changes in our lives that are self-initiated and lasting are almost always the result of a combination of external conditions *and* deep soul searching. We make choices based on self-examination and the circumstances surrounding our lives. Usually, in these cases, we are changed forever. We have created a new personal history with new challenges and possibilities.

It is this kind of change that this book is about and that makes process so important. For "doers" in a hurried, fast-paced world, nothing seems more counterintuitive than initiating a group whose purpose is to look at the assumptions that drive us and how those assumptions relate to the external reality of which we are a part. It seems like a waste of precious time. Ironically, though, purpose, direction, and initiated action take place. We understand ourselves as beings in process, whose purpose is to continually create ourselves.

The real, substantive changes in our lives that are self-initiated and lasting are almost always the result of a combination of external conditions and *deep soul searching.*

We three began this book with an emphasis on a theory of learning that has emerged from brain research. We believe this informs us with substantive understandings related to our tasks as educators. Through group process, we can integrate these understandings into our practice and the school culture. To help you extend your journey, however, into a landscape of possibility, we offer five guiding principles. These are applicable at both a classroom and a school level. The content of each has been discussed at length throughout this book, but setting them forth in this way may give you some landmarks for your journey.

1. **Create a purposeful, self-reflective environment.**

   This environment must include some common theoretical understandings and a commitment to explore assumptions and practice through group process.

2. **Embrace the possibilities of process and self-organization.**

   Within the environment there are multiple opportunities for interaction, community, and complex experience.

3. **Establish an environment that fosters, promotes, and celebrates creativity.**

   Such an environment allows individuals to explore their creative potentials and to learn from others as well.

4. **Commit to a practice of integrity and authenticity.**

   Such a practice means living our truth and being open to deeper exploration at the same time. It establishes trust and a willingness to work through inevitable misunderstandings and conflicts. It leads to self-efficacy and community.

5. **Affirm a sense of connectedness and honor the diversity that exists everywhere in our world.**

   Celebrate distinctions among personalities and cultures and be willing to hear their voices. Seek out our unity and our common human heritage.

In making this journey, proceed with a gentleness of spirit, acceptance rather than judgment, and compassion for one another. It is a long journey and each of us is a pioneer in a different perceptual world. It is important work. It matters.

What to "Unpack"

On most journeys, it is helpful to anticipate what to bring along to be prepared for changes in climate and geography. On this particular journey, however, we will find our expectations challenged more than anticipated. We may find ourselves in the position of unlearning before we can learn. Just like the porpoise in Bateson's experiment, we may have to look closely at what has to be discarded before we can move ahead. We three suspect that one of the notions that will need to change most dramatically is curriculum.

Most teachers tend to take curriculum for granted as that stuff that they are told they have to teach. Probably no aspect of schooling is so stuck in an old paradigm as our curriculum. As you become more creative; as you build from the interests and abilities of your students; as you delve more deeply into concepts, ideas, meanings, and purposes; and as you increasingly integrate real-life concerns into your classroom, the strain on the traditional understandings of curriculum and curriculum development will become greater and greater. This area is one in which we are only beginning to understand the significant implications of the new paradigm.

This journey will require us to respond in some way to the clash between what we do and our new sensibilities. As we confront our assumptions, our practice, and our learning environment, we will come to understand what responsive learning really means. Responsive learning suggests an education that itself is responsive to the needs of our time and an educational process that elicits and encourages a response from students.

An Education That "Responds"

Most of us began our careers in education with the thought of making a difference. We, like others before us, had a faith that education and learning can improve the lives of individuals and help make the world a better place. While our notions of education as a panacea may have been tempered, for many of us there is still an inclination to see our roles in terms of service. But schooling tends toward the accommodation of existing conditions. Maxine Greene (1989) calls this tendency the "inescapably there." We feel we must teach "what is" rather than "what might be."

Sam sometimes begins one of his classes with a question concerning the purpose of schooling. Inevitably an answer is given, with wide agreement, that schooling is meant to prepare students to take productive roles in society. Taking this assumption at face value, the class views selections of a remarkable film by Phillip Glass called *Koyaanisqatsi,* a Hopi word that is not satisfactorily translated into English. The film has no dialogue, only photographic images choreographed to dramatic and riveting music. It begins with beautiful images of the American Southwest and pictographs on cave walls. Accompanied by hauntingly beautiful chants and serene music, a sensory treat of color, natural harmony, and physical integration are offered viewers. As we view rock towers situated among a mixture of plains and distant mountains, the scene turns to the towering buildings of a large city. With speed photography and equally fast-paced music, we view ourselves in the settings that we have created. The fast motion allows us to watch ourselves from a new perspective. We are taken to our freeways, to our downtown streets, and inside offices and factories, malls and theaters. We see ourselves on escalators, being funneled along just like products on the assembly line. We watch ourselves as we consume products, eat at fast food centers, play video games, and relate casually. We also see the detached poor in our society, moments of tenderness and heroism, pictures of our pain and happiness. We are mesmerized by the mechanical nature of our lives and how unrelated they seem from the scenes at the beginning of the film. It is replete with our own technocratization. Finally, we are transported to a slow-motion visual account of the *Challenger* explosion, an emotional rendering of a horrible event. As this scene concludes, we return to the chanting sound of *koyaanisqatsi* amid the pictographs on cave walls. In silence we read that the word *koyaanisqatsi* means "out of balance, racing toward destruction." The film ends. The classroom is silent as students confront what "preparing students to take productive roles in society" really means. They had not considered that the phrase implies an acceptance of society as it is, ignoring aspects that may need to be reconsidered.

The paradox for all educators is that we are expected to prepare students for the society we have while we prepare them with skills and sensibilities to make it better. A daunting task. Explicitly we are to conserve and perpetuate; implicitly we are to revolutionize, or at least reform. Making this dialectic, or the tension between two possibilities, a part of our own professional lives invites us to consider the context of our practice in terms of its broader implications. Being willing to engage the world we live in and to see it as it is takes courage and insight. When we view it, however, not from an objectified view but rather as a world of which we are a part, there is an opening to freedom. We are not trying to obscure or hide, but we take it into ourselves as part of who we are. At this point, choice and decision become personal responses, not arguments and debates. An education that responds feels free to engage the world on its own terms and still to press forward the question "Could it be different and better?"

An Education That Elicits a "Response"

It is easy to feel the weight of external conditions and be overwhelmed. Whether in our personal lives or in the consideration of the social realities of our time, we experience the frustration of how huge and complicated problems may seem. You may find yourself sometimes switching the TV channel when one more story of poverty or environmental degradation comes on; it just hurts too much. Such downshifting can sometimes cause us to assume too quickly that we cannot make a difference. We negate the possibilities of who we might become and how we might respond. Christopher Lasch (1984) calls this condition "the minimal self" (59). We become overwhelmed by external circumstances, feel victimized and powerless. When we perceive education, however, as not just an activity that learns "about" something but empowers us to respond to our learning, then it becomes an active engagement of self-creation.

Responsiveness can help us elude an impotent nihilism in which nothing matters because it is too removed from us or outside of our control. Responding to our learning opens our whole self to the learning occasion. In the words of David Levin, when we "take to heart" what we know and what we see, we engage it with our whole being.

Tim Rollins, an art teacher at an intermediate school in the south Bronx, uses art with his students as a way to invite them to respond to what they were learning. Using literary selections, they explore comparisons between significant literary themes and their own lives. Books such as Dickens's *Hard Times*, Kafka's *Amerika*, Dante's *Inferno* are used to trigger correspondences to and images of today's life. The students spend a great deal of time honing the symbols and images that are most significant to them. They explore not only the world of literature but also the world they live in, seeing it with new perspectives. These students' work is featured in galleries and museums in this country and abroad. Through their learning, they make a difference. Learning that elicits a response is contemplative, in that we go within ourselves to discover what response is appropriate, and it is active as we create a space in the world that shares our "new self" with others.

Education that brings us into response calls us forth in relationship with ourselves and the world. It is a response into relationship that we three are talking about, where people become active and responsive to our place in the world. We start from where we are, bringing forth ourselves into the space of real events. Education in this sense helps us to "know" and gives us the opportunity to "be."

> *You are what your deep, driving desire is.*
> *As your desire is, so is your will.*
> *As your will is, so is your deed.*
> *As your deed is, so is your destiny.*
>
> —Upanishads

Responsive Learning as Identity and Being

When we understand dynamical knowledge as that knowing which becomes part of us, then we can see that responsive learning becomes part of our very identity. Responsive learning assumes that who we are makes a difference in the world. It assumes that in a related and interconnected world our thoughts, actions, and sensitivities make a difference. It assumes that our own expressive voices are to be honored and used for more than mere ego satisfaction, as extensions into the world of which we are part. Our individuality is protected even as our broader connections to the world are honored.

Our colleague Todd Jennings (1996) conducted some fascinating interviews with persons who were active volunteers in helping others, some in many parts of the world and at great personal sacrifice. What he learned was that these individuals have created an extended identity of self. In other words, they do not see themselves as separate from those they serve.

They do not experience feelings of defeat or see themselves powerless in the face of sometimes overwhelming conditions. They live who they are. Jennings's work suggests to us that responsive learning is deeply connected to our identity of self. It also suggests that our sense of self is related to the connectedness we perceive in the world.

Certainly authentic assessments are some initial ways to encourage individual responses to what students learn. Use of multiple intelligences in the curriculum provides variety, diversity, and personal options. Voluntary service opportunities for students broaden the application of their learning. Our own notion of active processing opens us to creative and far-reaching approaches to understanding and responding. We suspect, though, that these are only touching the surface of the possibilities of what responsive learning might or could mean.

Amid this possibility of greater challenge, we all are faced with our own responses, our own identities, and our own "where we go from here." Educating as if the world matters begins with a new perception of possibility. Orientation Three thinking thrusts us forth into new ways of being and acting in the world and in our classrooms. We hope that your journey is as exciting as ours and that at some point we can share a common moment.

The Reenchantment of Learning

We end where we began. The cycle completes itself from beginning to end, only to begin again. We are part of the natural processes of the world and part of our legacy is to participate creatively in the unfolding of life. The ordinary is full of wonder and mystery. There is an inherent joy in opening to this wonder, to sensing our connection to it, and in seeing ourselves as more than a single entity.

Children
of the earth,
come out
of the darkness—
light your candles
from the stars . . .
Keep vigil
for all the world.
Let no heart
deny the other . . .
let your love
be the sign of peace
made visible.

—Stephanie Chase

Process and Reflections

Personal

1. This chapter consolidates some of the major points of the book. Using a journal, spend some time revisiting parts of the book and you own experiences of working through it. What stands out to you as significant? What experiences stand out in your mind? How will you respond to your knowing?

Group

1. Using the group process, describe your vision of the teacher you want to be. Describe the qualities of a school that would support that vision.
2. Building upon the journey metaphor used in this chapter, discuss possibilities at your school. Keep the discussion at the level of possibility for this exercise. How will you map your journey? What must you unlearn in order to succeed?
3. Where do you go from here?
4. Make plans to continue the group process and create a celebration that brings this phase of growth to an end. Beginnings and endings create a cycle and are found everywhere in life.

We hope that this book has engaged your thinking as well as your spirit. Again we invite you to work through the book individually as well as in groups in which the collective power of community can support and guide you.

If you wish to share with us your thoughts and ideas about this book or your journey to reenchantment, we would love to hear from you. You may reach us at P. O. Box 1511, Idyllwild, CA 92549. Sam's e-mail address is scrowell@wiley.csusb.edu

Appendix

Group Process

The group process is the foundation of our learning communities. It is referred to throughout the book and is discussed at length in chapter 8. We invite you to organize process groups at your school and to work through this book together. We believe that through individual and group reflection, natural change that is purposeful, meaningful, and substantive can occur.

Membership

The ideal size of the group is six to ten people who commit to meeting on a regular basis. Ideally, membership is across functions, divisions, and positions so that many of the participants do not know one another or work closely together. This diversity introduces an essential element of novelty and variety.

Meetings

Meetings are intended to last between one-and-a-half and two hours and ideally should be held every week. If possible, participants should meet in some part of the school that they do not regularly use for work. Some teachers we work with meet in their homes. As much as possible, avoid comings and goings during the meetings.

Protocols

Although there is substantial room for creativity and personal choice, we have found that groups succeed when the members adhere to a basic set of routines and procedures.

1. Beginning and ending on time

Punctuality is important because it contributes both to orderliness and to trust. As there is so much about restructuring that is uncertain, some core protocols that everyone can rely on become very important. Commitment to beginning and ending on time is a little frustrating for some people, but is extremely valuable to most participants.

2. Starting with a simple and accepted procedure that gives everyone a moment to relax

When people come to the group, their minds are still full of the events of the day and of the problems that they have to solve. We suggest that the group members find some way to relax their minds and to bring their attention to bear on the group itself. There is no limit to the methods that may be used. A few moments of silence is one method. A short relaxation exercise is another.

Ordered Sharing

Ordered sharing is perhaps most powerful in generating the spirit that we seek. Following are the steps to conducting a successful ordered sharing session:

1. Sit in a closed circle. A closed circle eliminates hierarchy and engenders a sense of equality.
2. Agree upon some core material to read or explore. Ideally the material should be some big idea or pithy saying that applies across the board and that is open to multiple interpretations and points of view. Because there are so many legitimate points of view, there is something to which everyone can relate personally. At the same time, the range of possibilities fosters open-minded listening. Some ideas that we use, in part because they begin to make sense of the notion of wholeness and connectedness, follow:

   - *Everything is separate and connected.*
   - *Whatever is, is always in process.*

- *The whole is greater than the sum of the parts.*
- *The whole is present in the part.*
- *Order is present everywhere.*
- *Everything comes in layers.*
- *There is always more than meets the eye.*
- *Inside and outside reflect each other.*

3. Ask participants to take a moment to reflect on the reading or quotation. This time is *not* a time to search for what it "really" means, but an opportunity to think about what it currently means to each participant.
4. Individually, express a personal thought, experience, or insight about the quotation with a time limit of, perhaps, one or two minutes. The person to the left or right of the speaker expresses an opinion next. The direction of sharing continues around the circle. Although some might feel that this is awkward and counterintuitive at first, you will begin to be very comfortable with it. It eliminates competition for time and space, and it ensures that each person will have precisely the same opportunity to speak and to listen. It also sets the stage for the in-depth communication that is ultimately the goal for the group. No one makes any comment whatsoever about what another says. There is no opposition, nor is there verbal support. Every silent member pays full attention to what is being said. The reason for the silence and for the absence of feedback is to provide legitimacy for whatever opinion a person expresses. Such silence is a way of giving people permission to hold and express their opinions.
5. The group leader for the meeting monitors timing and participation, which means he or she has the responsibility for calling "time" when the allocated time for any person to speak has expired. The group leader also monitors the ordered sharing around the circle. Should it be necessary, he or she may ask anyone who keeps on making comments to refrain from doing so, but maintaining the integrity of the process should really be the responsibility of all the participants.
6. Reflect briefly and in silence upon what was said and upon your own reactions to the content and the process.
7. If everyone agrees, repeat the process. However, it is not an intensive experience in any one session that matters, but the repetition of the process every week.

8. Move to the next phase of the group meeting without discussion. This step is often extremely difficult for people, whose basic predilection is to jump into discussion and debate. However, this process is set up precisely to generate a different sense of being together, a sense in which debate, immediate advocacy, and defense of a position are not the objectives. We therefore ask participants simply to move on to the next aspect of the group meeting without further exploring the topic.

Comment

The procedure we describe may take no more than ten minutes, though it can take as long as twenty. It is possible in workshops and other settings to practice several times over a period of, say, two days. However, we have found that simply implementing this procedure diligently for a few minutes every week is sufficient to have a very powerful effect.

Bibliography

Alexander, C. N., and E. J. Langer, Eds. 1990. *Higher State of Human Development*. New York: Oxford Press.

Andrews, D. 1966. *Symphony of Life*. Lee's Summit, Mo.: Unity.

Bandura, A. 1992. "Self-Efficacy Mechanism in Sociocognitive Functioning." Presentation at the annual meeting of the American Educational Research Association, San Francisco. April.

Bateson, G. 1974. *Steps to an Ecology of Mind*. New York: Balentine.

Berman, M. 1981. *The Reenchantment of the World*. Ithaca, N.Y.: Cornell UP.

Berry, T. 1990. *The Dream of the Earth*. San Francisco: Sierra Club.

Bohm, D. 1982. "The Enfolding-Unfolding Universe." In *The Holographic Paradigm and Other Paradoxes: Exploring the Leading Edge of Science*, edited by K. Wilber. Boulder, Colo.: Shambhala.

Bohm, D., and F. D. Peat. 1987. *Science, Order, and Creativity*. New York: Boynton.

Bopp, J., M. Bopp, Lee Brown, and Phil Lane. 1989. *The Sacred Tree: Reflections on Native American Spirituality*. Twin Lakes, Wis.: Bantam.

Bransford, D., and M. Johnson. 1972. "Contextual Prerequisites for Understanding: Some Investigations of Comprehensive Recall." *Journal of Verbal Learning and Verbal Behavior* 11: 717–21.

Briggs, J., and F. D. Peat. 1984. *Looking Glass Universe: The Emerging Science of Wholeness*. New York: Simon and Schuster.

Caine, R. N., and G. Caine. 1994. *Making Connections: Teaching and the Human Brain*. Rev. ed. Menlo Park, Calif.: Addison-Wesley.

———. 1997a. *Education on the Edge of Possibility*. Alexandria, Va.: ASCD.

———. 1997b. *Unleashing the Power of Perceptual Change: The Promise of Brain-Based Teaching*. Alexandria, Va.: ASCD.

Caine, G., R. N. Caine, and S. Crowell. 1994. *MindShifts: A Brain-Based Process for Restructuring Schools and Renewing Education*. Tucson, Ariz.: Zephyr Press.

Cameron, J. 1992. *The Artist's Way*. New York: G. P. Putnam's.

Campbell, J. 1988. *The Inner Reaches of Outer Space: Metaphor as Myth and Religion*. New York: Harper.

———. 1989. *The Improbable Machine*. New York: Simon and Schuster.

Capra, F. 1982. *The Turning Point: Science, Society, and the Rising Culture*. New York: Bantam.

———. 1991. *The Tao of Physics*. Rev. ed. Boston: Shambhala.

Cohen, E. 1994. *Designing Groupwork: Strategies for the Heterogeneous Classroom*. New York: Teachers College Press.

Combs, A. W., A. C. Richards, and F. Richards. 1988. *Perceptual Psychology*. Landham, Md.: University Press of America.

Combs, A. W., and D. Snygg. 1959. *Individual Behavior: A Perceptual Approach to Behavior*. New York: Harper and Row.

Crowell, S. 1989. "A New Way of Thinking: The Challenge of the Future." *Educational Leadership* 47, 1: 60.

Crowell, S. 1995. "Landscapes of Change: Toward a New Paradigm for Education." In *Integrative Learning as a Pathway to Teaching Holism, Complexity, and Interconnectedness*, edited by B. Blair and R. Caine. Lewiston, N.Y.: Edwin Mellen Press.

Crowell, S., and R. N. Caine. 1997. "Restructuring as an Integrative Process." In *Restructuring for Integrative Education*, edited by Todd Jennings. Westpoint, Conn.: Bergin and Garvey.

Csikszentmihalyi, M. 1990. *Flow: The Psychology of Optimal Experience*. New York: Harper Perennial.

Davies, P. 1988. *The Cosmic Blueprint: New Discoveries in Nature's Ability to Order the Universe*. New York: Simon and Schuster.

Doll, W. E. 1993. *A Post-Modern Perspective on Curriculum*. New York: Teachers College Press.

Drucker, P. 1969. *The Age of Discontinuity: Guidelines to Our Changing Society*. New York: Harper and Row.

Dubos, R. 1971. *The God Within*. New York: Charles Scribner.

Elgin, D. 1993. *Voluntary Simplicity*. New York: William Morrow.

Fields, R. 1984. *Chop Wood, Carry Water: A Guide to Finding Spiritual Fulfillment in Everyday Life*. Los Angeles: Jeremy P. Tarcher.

Fuller, R. B. 1979. *R. Buckminster Fuller on Education*. Amherst, Mass.: University of Massachusetts Press.

Gablik, S. 1993. *The Reenchantment of Art*. London: Thames and Hudson.

Gang, Philip S., Nina M. Lynn, and Dorothy Maver. 1992. *Conscious Education: The Bridge to Freedom*. Atlanta, Ga.: Dagaz Press.

Gardner, H. 1993. *Frames of Mind: The Theory of Multiple Intelligences*. Rev. ed. New York: Basic.

Garmston, R.. and B. Wellman. 1995. Adaptive Schools in a Quantum Universe." *Educational Leadership* 52, 7: 6.

Gilbert, A. G. 1997. "Movement Is the Key to Learning." *Mindshift Connection* February: 10–11.

Goerner, S. 1994. *Chaos and the Evolving Ecological Universe*. Langhorne, Pa.: Gordon and Breach.

Goldberg, N. 1990. *Wild Mind: Living the Writer's Life*. New York: Bantam.

Greene, M. 1988. *The Dialectic of Freedom*. New York: Teachers College Press.

Griffin, D. R., ed. 1990. *Sacred Interconnection: Postmodern Spirituality, Political Economy, and Art*. New York: SUNY Press.

Grigg, R. 1990. *The Tao of Being*. Atlanta, Ga.: Humanics.

Halgren, E. , C. L. Wilson, N. K. Squires, J. Engel, R. D. Walter, and P. H. Crandall. 1983. "Dynamics of the Hippocampal Contribution to Memory: Stimulation and Recording Studies in Humans." In *Molecular, Cellular, and Behavioral Neurobiology of the Hippocampus*, edited by W. Seifert. New York: Academic Press.

Hand, J. D. 1984. "Split Brain Theory and Recent Results in Brain Research: Implications for the Design of Instruction." In *Instructional Development: The State of the Art*, vol. 2, edited by R. K. Bass and C. R. Dills. Dubuque, Iowa: Kendall/Hunt.

Harmon, W. 1988. "The Postmodern Heresy: Consciousness as Causal." In *The Reenchantment of Science: Postmodern Proposals*, edited by David Ray Griffin. Albany, N.Y.: SUNY Press.

Hart, L. A. 1975. *How the Brain Works: A New Understanding of Human Learning, Emotion, and Thinking*. New York: Basic Books.

———. 1983. *Human Brain, Human Learning*. New York: Longman.

Herrigel, E. 1989. *Zen in the Art of Archery*. Rev. ed. New York: Vintage.

Isaacs, W. N. 1993. "Taking Flight: Dialogue, Collective Thinking, and Organizational Learning." *Organizational Systems* 22: 24–39.

Itten, J. 1975. *Design and Form*. New York: Reinhold.

Jacobs, W. J., and L. Nadel. 1985. "Stress-Induced Recovery of Fears and Phobias." *Psychological Review* 92, 4: 512–31.

Jantsch, E. 1980. *The Self-Organizing Universe: Scientific and Human Implications of the Emerging Paradigm of Evolution*. Oxford: Pergamon Press.

Jennings, T. 1996. "The Developmental Dialectic of International Human Rights Advocacy." *Political Psychology*. 17, 1: 77–96.

Kelly, K. 1994. *Out of Control: The New Biology of Machines, Social Systems, and the Economic World.* New York: Addison-Wesley.

Kuhn, T. 1962. *The Structure of Scientific Revolution.* Chicago: University of Chicago Press.

Lakoff, G. 1987. *Women, Fire, and Dangerous Things.* Chicago: University of Chicago Press.

Langer, E. 1989. *Mindfulness.* Reading, Mass.: Addison-Wesley.

Lasch, C. 1984. *The Minimal Self: Psychic Survival in Troubled Times.* New York: W. W. Norton.

Leonard, G., and M. Murphy. 1995. *The Life We Are Given.* New York: Jeremy Tarcher.

Levin, O. 1989. *The Listening Self: Personal Growth, Social Change, and the Closure of Metaphysics.* Boston: MIT Press.

Levy, B. 1972. "Do Teachers Sell Girls Short?" *Today's Education* 61: 27–29.

Lyons, J. 1997. "The Dramatic Classroom." *Mindshift Bulletin* February: 3.

Mcguinness, D., and K. Pribram. 1980. "The Neuropsychology of Attention: Emotional and Motivational Controls." In *The Brain and Psychology,* edited by M. D. Wittrock. New York: Academic Press.

Miller, John P. 1988. *The Holistic Curriculum.* Toronto: OISE Press.

Moore, T. 1992. *In Care of the Soul.* New York: HarperCollins.

Morris, D. 1962. *The Biology of Art.* London: Methuen.

Nadel, L., and J. Wilmer. 1980. "Context and Conditioning: A Place for Space." *Physiological Psychology* 8: 218–28.

Nadel, L., J. Wilmer, and E. M. Kurz. 1984. "Cognitive Maps and Environmental Context." In *Context and Learning,* edited by P. Balsam and A. Tomi. Hillsdale, N.J.: Lawrence Erlbaum.

Needleman, J. 1982. *The Heart of Philosophy.* New York: Alfred A. Knopf.

Neilhardt, J. 1972. *Black Elk Speaks.* Rev. ed. New York: MJF Books.

O'Keefe, J., and L. Nadel. 1978. *The Hippocampus as a Cognitive Map.* New York: Oxford UP.

Oliver, D. 1989. *Education, Modernity, and Fractured Meaning: Toward a Process Theory of Teaching and Learning.* Albany, N.Y.: SUNY Press.

Ornstein, R., and D. Sobel. 1987. *The Healing Brain: Breakthrough Discoveries about How the Brain Keeps Us Healthy.* New York: Simon and Schuster.

Percy, W. 1959. *The Message in the Bottle.* New York: Farrar, Straus, and Giroux.

Perkins, D. 1995. *Outsmarting IQ: The Emerging Science of Learnable Intelligence.* New York: The Free Press.

Poplin, M. 1984. "Toward an Holistic View of Persons with Learning Disabilities." *Learning Disability Quarterly* 7:

Prigogine, I., and I. Stengers. 1984. *Order Out of Chaos: Man's New Dialogue with Nature.* New York: Bantam.

Rogers, C. 1969. *Freedom to Learn.* Columbus, Ohio: Charles E. Merrill.

Rosenfield, I. 1988. *The Invention of Memory.* New York: Basic.

Springer, S. and G. Deutsch. 1985. *Left Brain, Right Brain.* 2nd ed. New York: W. H. Freeman.

Somé, M. 1995. *Of Water and Spirit.* New York: Arkana.

Toulmin, S. E. 1982. *The Return to Cosmology: Post-Modern Science and the Theology of Nature.* Berkeley, Calif.: University of California Press.

Vaill, P. 1996. *Learning as a Way of Being.* San Francisco: Jossey Bass.

Poplin, M., and J. Weeres, eds. 1992. *Voices from the Inside.* Claremont, Calif.: Claremont Graduate School.

Waldrop, M. M. 1992. *Complexity: The Emerging Science at the Edge of Order and Chaos.* New York: Simon and Schuster.

Webster's New World Dictionary of the American Language. 1960. Cleveland, Ohio: The World Publishing Company.

Wheatley, M. 1992. *Leadership and the New Science: Learning about Organization from an Orderly Universe.* San Francisco: Berrett-Koehler.

Wheatley, M., and M. Kellner-Rogers. 1996. *A Simpler Way.* San Francisco: Berrett-Koehler.

Whitehead, A. N. 1967. *The Aims of Education.* New York: Free Press.